WILLIAMS-SONOMA

desserts
new healthy kitchen

RECIPES
Annabel Langbein

GENERAL EDITOR
Chuck Williams

PHOTOGRAPHY
Dan Goldberg & Ben Dearnley

fP
FREE PRESS

NEW YORK · LONDON · TORONTO · SYDNEY

contents

About this book

The books in the New Healthy Kitchen series offer simple and appealing ways to enjoy a diet rich in fruits, vegetables, and grains.

We are blessed with an abundance of food, from superb raw ingredients to highly processed convenience foods, but it's easy to get stuck in a food rut or make unhealthy choices. Since the foods you eat directly affect your overall health and your energy level, incorporating a wide selection of fresh produce and whole grains into your diet and cooking food yourself are two of the best things you can do to eat both healthfully and well.

The recipes in *Desserts* are organized in a new way: by the color of the fruits and vegetables used in the dishes. A chapter on whole grains, nuts, and seeds rounds out the book with appealing ways to enjoy such supremely wholesome foods. This accessible and informative approach shows how each color group contributes different benefits to your health. Thinking about the color of foods is an easy way to make sure you're consuming all the fresh produce you need. If you remember to eat at least one fruit or vegetable from each color group daily, as part of a meal, as a snack, and for dessert, you are well on your way to enjoying a varied and nutritious diet.

The New Healthy Kitchen series will bring color and creativity into your kitchen while helping you to use a wide variety of fresh produce and whole grains in your meals every day.

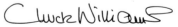

Eating the rainbow

Purple and blue fruits and vegetables contain fiber, vitamins, and phytochemicals that promote heart health; help memory function; lower the risk of some cancers; promote urinary tract health; and boost immunity

White and tan fruits and vegetables contain fiber, vitamins, and phytochemicals that promote heart health; help maintain healthful cholesterol levels; lower the risk of breast, lung, and other cancers; and slow cholesterol absorption

Green fruits and vegetables contain fiber, vitamins, and phytochemicals that lower the risk of breast, prostate, lung, and other cancers; promote eye health; help build strong bones and teeth; and boost immunity

Red fruits and vegetables contain fiber, vitamins, and phytochemicals that promote heart health; help memory function; lower the risk of some cancers; promote urinary tract health; and boost immunity

Brown whole grains, legumes, seeds, and nuts include fiber, vitamins, and phytonutrients that lower blood cholesterol levels and reduce the risk of colon and other cancers, diabetes, heart disease, and stroke

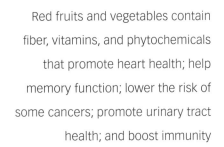

Yellow and orange fruits and vegetables contain fiber, vitamins, and phytochemicals that promote heart health; promote eye health; lower the risk of some cancers; and boost immunity

Adapted from educational materials of the Produce for Better Health Foundation

The new healthy kitchen

Popular diet regimes often focus on forbidding or restricting certain foods. Cut out all fat. Avoid carbs. Eat lots of grapefruit, or nothing but cabbage soup. Despite the promises of such fads, nutritionists are growing ever more certain that what we truly need for optimum health is variety. Our bodies require a number of essential nutrients, and the best way to get them is to eat a wide range of fresh foods.

The New Healthy Kitchen series takes the approach that healthful food is good, fresh food, simply prepared to bring out its appealing flavors and beautifully presented to delight the senses. For desserts, this means starting with high-quality ingredients, especially fresh fruits, a variety of nuts, dark chocolate, and the occasional wholesome grain, and preparing them with an eye to preserving their inherent colors and textures as well as

their valuable nutrients. The recipes in this healthy cookbook emphasize freshness, color, flavor, and variety.

Our bodies need the vitamins, minerals, and fiber provided by a wide range of plant foods in order to stay healthy. In addition to supplying these essentials, fruits, vegetables, and grains are also rich in phytochemicals, beneficial compounds found only in plants. In many cases, the phytochemicals are what

give fruits and vegetables their vibrant colors and distinctive flavors. They also help our bodies fight off disease and damage.

Unfortunately, our modern diet is remarkably limited in the kind of plant foods we eat. With the abundance of all types of food at our disposal, we tend to overindulge in concentrated sources of energy, especially animal fats. We also gravitate toward carbohydrates, which are excellent sources of

quick energy; however, some common carbohydrates, such as refined flours, are stripped of the wholesome nutrients found in the whole grains.

Popping pills and taking supplements aren't the best solutions to a lack of vitamins and minerals in the diet. Allowing your body to extract these nutrients from different foods is the very best way of getting what you need, in the natural form in which your body is designed to use it.

Current nutritional guidelines recommend eating at least four servings of fruit each day, plus five servings of vegetables. A serving is not large, but to ensure that you get a wide range of nutrients, you should vary the fruits and vegetables you eat. This cookbook offers many delicious ways to include fruit in your meals each day. Additionally, a good portion of the food you eat daily should come from grains, nuts, and seeds. These foods are rich in fiber, protein, and minerals. While whole grains play only a small role in sweet dishes, it's hard to imagine desserts without nuts and two other well-loved seeds: the coffee bean and the cocoa bean.

Paying attention to the color of ingredients when you prepare desserts will help you remember to bring a wide variety of bright, ripe produce into your diet. Keeping the focus on color also increases the benefits to your health, since each color of fruit, from red cherries to green grapes to yellow lemons, provides different health-enhancing phyto-chemicals. To help you enjoy all the wonderful plant foods that can play a role in an after-dinner treat, the chapters in this book are organized by the five prominent color groups of fresh produce: purple and blue, green, white and tan, yellow and orange, and red. A sixth chapter focuses on the "brown" ingredients: whole grains, nuts, and seeds, including coffee and chocolate.

Each produce chapter begins with a chart showing which fruits are at their peak of ripeness each season. The Brown chapter chart shows which grains, legumes, nuts, and seeds might figure in a delicious dessert. The recipes themselves are simple and straightforward, designed for real-life cooks who haven't much time to spare, but want to use the time they do have to prepare healthful, colorful, and, above all, delicious foods for themselves and their families.

Fruits & vegetables

Fresh produce is one of the foundations of a healthy diet. Fruits, in particular, are some of the most beautiful foods on the planet—a gift to all the senses, with vibrant colors, heady perfumes, and flavors that range from tart to sweet. Many fruits are appealing enough to serve as a treat when simply eaten out of hand, and the sweetness inherent in some vegetables can make for a wonderful dessert.

In the early years of the twentieth century, researchers discovered that fruits and vegetables contain the various vitamins and minerals we now know are essential to maintaining good health and fighting disease. We are now entering into a similarly exciting era of discovery, as we learn about the roles that phytochemicals play in our bodies.

These protective compounds found in plants, believed to number in the thousands, work alone and in combination with one another and with nutrients. They work in different ways. For example, some phytochemicals act as antioxidants, which protect the body by neutralizing unstable oxygen molecules (known as free radicals) that damage cells and promote disease. Eating plant foods rich in antioxidants can reduce the incidence of various cancers, heart disease, impaired vision, and other health problems. Fruits and vegetables from each of the color groups provide us with their own unique combination of phytonutrients, each playing its own role in fighting disease and promoting health.

By eating a wide variety of fruits and vegetables at their peak of ripeness, you will not only please your palate, but you will also give your body the benefit of all the healthy nutrients that these foods contain.

Grains & seeds

Grains, which are the seeds of plants, contain a wealth of nutrients. They are rich in vitamins and minerals, protein, and fiber, all of which are essential to a healthful diet. Whole grains don't make many appearances at dessert time, but they should not be discounted altogether. For the sweet purposes of this book, they can be grouped with a few other beneficial seeds: nuts, coffee, and chocolate.

Like vegetables and fruits, grains contain beneficial phytochemicals in addition to a number of essential nutrients. When a grain is refined—as when wheat is made into white flour—the fiber-rich hull and the nutrient-rich germ are removed, leaving the endosperm, which is largely starch. Although white flour and other refined grains are often enriched with a few nutrients that have been removed in milling, important components like fiber and phytochemicals are not replaced. As a result, eating refined grains, as well as refined sugars, raises the blood sugar level and upsets the body's balance. By contrast, eating whole grains can help maintain healthful cholesterol levels.

Nuts, another type of plant seed, are rich in omega-3 fatty acids, substances that are essential to brain function and also good for the heart. Nuts are also loaded with fiber, which helps maintain low cholesterol levels, and with vitamin E, an antioxidant linked to decreased risk of heart disease.

Two other seed-based foods, coffee and chocolate, are of special interest in a dessert cookbook. They may not seem like health foods, but both offer a number of valuable health benefits. Coffee is packed with antioxidants, as well as minerals such as magnesium. Cocoa beans, a primary ingredient in chocolate, contain more than six hundred plant chemicals, including anti-oxidants such as catechins, which are also found in fruits, vegetables, and red wine. The darker the chocolate, the better: milk chocolate has a lower percentage of chocolate liquor from cocoa beans and more added sugar as well as milk.

The Brown chapter celebrates the virtues of eating desserts made with coffee and dark chocolate. It also provides delicious ways to enjoy whole grains and several varieties of nuts. White flour is usually the grain of choice for desserts, but whole grains can make desserts more interesting and satisfying. Combining these foods with fruits will make the finale of your meal as satisfying and appealing as the main course.

Other ingredients

The New Healthy Kitchen philosophy is to eat a wide variety of wholesome foods, rather than to limit what you eat. The mainstays of your diet should be fruits and vegetables, with an emphasis on whole grains and legumes as well. While fat and sugar should make up just a small percentage of the food you eat, they are essential in many desserts. Enjoying them in moderation is the key.

The flavor and texture of a pastry crust is not the same without sweet butter, and cheese makes a delicious partner for many fruits. Even when a dessert is somewhat rich, it is more wholesome if you prepare it yourself using high-quality, fresh ingredients rather than serve packaged sweets that contain artificial additives and preservatives. Some of the desserts in *Desserts* are luxurious. (Nutritional analyses on pages 130–33 will

help you determine how rich a particular dessert is.) In these cases, keep in mind that a little goes a long way. Enjoy a rich treat, but cut slender slices and save leftovers for another day instead of offering seconds. Even for desserts made with fruits and other healthy ingredients, a serving is not as generous as you may think. When you know that dessert is on the day's menu, eat a lighter lunch or dinner than you normally would.

The desserts in *Desserts* include dairy in the form of milk and cream, cheese, yogurt, sour cream and crème fraîche, and butter. When choosing these ingredients, especially milk and yogurt, look for organic products, as they have the best flavor. Two-percent milk, low-fat yogurt, and light sour cream can be used in most desserts if the whole versions are too heavy for you. (If best flavor and texture is your main concern, try whole fat.)

Nonfat and one-percent dairy products will not work as well in most cakes and other baked items. Always choose unsalted butter for fresher flavor and so that you can control the amount of salt in your cooking.

Eggs play another essential role in making desserts. Depending on how they are treated, they can help create the airy texture of a soufflé or meringue, the smooth richness of a flan or ice cream, or the moist crumb of a cake. A few years ago, eggs were regarded with suspicion from a health standpoint because of their cholesterol content, but this view has shifted as researchers learn more about how the body processes cholesterol. Eggs are now considered a highly nutritious part of a healthy diet, and eating eggs may even reduce the risk of heart disease and stroke, among other benefits.

While uncooked fruits at their seasonal peak need minimal sweetening, cooked fruit desserts regularly call for some kind of sweetener. Whenever possible, use unrefined sweeteners like maple syrup and unfiltered honey. Both make a particularly good glaze for grilled fruits. Flavorful honeys, like wildflower or lavender, can transform a bowl of perfectly ripe fresh fruit and plain yogurt into an after-dinner treat. In recipes that call for sugar, you can use organic granulated sugar or powdered (icing) sugar, both of which are available in natural foods stores. Turbinado sugar, raw sugar that has been cleaned by steaming, has a coarse texture and tan color that make it a delightful condiment sprinkled over sliced raw fruit.

Acidic ingredients can bring out a fruit's flavor without making a dessert heavy. Add a little lemon juice and/or zest to almost any cooked fruit dessert, from an apple crisp to a winter fruit compote, and taste to see how it intensifies the fruit's flavor. Even vinegars boost the taste of fruits; try raspberry vinegar with sugar on peaches, or the classic Italian combination of aged balsamic vinegar and freshly ground black pepper sprinkled on the ripest strawberries (page 101).

Liqueurs, wine, and some spirits such as rum also complement and intensify the flavor of many fruits—and red wine in particular contributes heart-healthy phytonutrients. Many spices marry beautifully with fruit, especially cinnamon, nutmeg, cardamom, and mace. While mint is a classic flavoring or garnish for fruit, other fresh herbs, such as lavender, basil, thyme, and rosemary, give fruit desserts an ineffable, unique taste.

Creating the healthy dessert

Cooking at home is the best way to ensure that your food tastes good, retains as many nutrients as possible, and doesn't include additives you don't need. But the time it takes to plan, shop for, and prepare homemade meals is increasingly scarce as our lives become ever more complex. Luckily, the New Healthy Kitchen is designed for real-life cooks with real-life schedules.

Each recipe begins by noting the amount of time needed to prepare and cook it, so you can better plan the time it takes to create a homemade dessert. The "Fresh Ideas" in each chapter describe simple after-dinner dishes that are easier to make than going out to buy similar prepared desserts. During your busy day, you may be able to snack

on colorful fresh and dried fruits, but the evening meal is a good opportunity to use the recipes in *Desserts,* which allow you to include foods from all the color groups in the healthy-eating rainbow. You can plan your meals not just by what is available in the market, but also by the color of the main ingredient in each course. When combined,

the courses will make a colorful menu from starter to dessert. Your plates and table will be colorful, and your menu healthful.

Fruit is the perfect dessert to follow any recipe in the *Main Dishes* book of the New Healthy Kitchen series. Whether whole and raw or cooked into an elegant tart, fruit aids the digestion and doesn't overwhelm the palate or overfill the stomach. Just as you balance colors by including a range in your menu, you can balance strong flavors with mild. Fruit desserts are the perfect finale to a meaty main course, as their sweetness complements beef, pork, and lamb, as well as rich duck. A fruit sorbet is an ideal follow-up to a spicy main dish. Citrus-based desserts, such as Silky Lime Mousse (page 42) and Lemon Soufflés (page 86), are particularly good after a meal that includes fish.

The desserts in the New Healthy Kitchen range from grilled pineapple glazed with honey and flavored with star anise (page 76) to elegant lavender-infused flans garnished with plums (page 24). Among the baked goods are Blackberry Crumble (page 23),

Walnut & Date Tart (page 124), and Oatmeal Pear Crisp (page 123). While most of the desserts in *Desserts* are fruit based, vege-tables make an appearance too—in Carrot Cupcakes (page 82) and Chocolate-Pumpkin Cake (page 120). Grains such oatmeal and cornmeal are used in toppings and crusts.

As the recipes in *Desserts* make clear, eating healthfully is not about sacrifice or denial, but about moderation. Small amounts of added sweeteners intensify the natural sweetness of fruits, vegetables, and nuts, while a little butter rounds out the taste of a dessert and makes it more satisfying.

The preparation and cooking techniques used in *Desserts* range from simply cutting up and seasoning fresh fruit to making

easy mousses and sorbets. The glossary in the back of the book lists all the fresh ingredients used in the recipes and provides information on how to judge ripeness, where to seek out produce, and how to store fruit when you bring it home.

Finally, when you don't have the time or inclination to make a dessert, take a hint from the cuisines of the Near East, South-east Asia, and the Mediterranean, and serve whole fruit. Nature, with the help of plant breeders and growers, has already done most of the work for you, creating beautifully colored and uniquely shaped foods for you to enjoy. Savoring the pure taste of fresh fruit is a delicious, healthful, and fitting end to any healthy meal.

purple figs dried black currants

PURPLE AND BLUE FRUITS AND VEGETABLES PROMOTE

raisins blackberries blue grapes

MEMORY FUNCTION • HELP PROMOTE URINARY TRACT

blue plums fresh black currants

HEALTH • BOOST THE IMMUNE SYSTEM • HELP PROMOTE

prunes lavender purple grapes

HEALTHY AGING • OFFER ANTIOXIDANTS FOR HEALING

blueberries black plums purple

AND PROTECTION • HELP REDUCE THE RISK OF SOME

figs raisins dried black currants

CANCERS • PURPLE AND BLUE FRUITS AND VEGETABLES

Purple & blue

For many people—especially nutritional scientists—purple and blue are favorite colors. The list of the fruits in this group is short, but they constitute some of the most luscious and appealing produce available. They are also among the richest in disease-fighting antioxidants. Blueberries, in particular, have been studied extensively for their ability to improve memory and brain function.

Blackberries, which share many of the characteristics of blueberries, grow wild on brambles in many regions, just waiting for you to harvest them in late summer. Use them to make a simple crumble (page 23).

Ripe summer plums are prized by the French, especially the purple-black prune plum used to make the dried version. Plums are packed with nutrients as well as fiber. In the summertime, try ending a meal with simple and delicious baked plums (page 28).

You might think of purple grapes as a treat more than a health food, but grapes contain many of the same heart-healthy compounds as red wine. Use purple grapes to make an elegant tart (page 34).

Lavender flowers are edible and delicious, and have a phytochemical profile similar to that of blue fruits. Flavoring a simple custard with lavender (page 24) is a unique way to add a new blue ingredient to your meals.

Many blue fruits peak in the warm months. But even in midwinter, you can enjoy them in their flavorful dried forms.

SPRING	SUMMER	AUTUMN	WINTER
blueberries	blackberries	blueberries	dried black currants
fresh black currants	blueberries	dried black currants	blue, purple, or black grapes
blue, purple, or black grapes	fresh black currants	purple figs	prunes
blue, purple, or black plums	purple figs	blue, purple, or black grapes	raisins
prunes	blue, purple, or black grapes	blue, purple, or black plums	
raisins	lavender	prunes	
	blue, purple, or black plums	raisins	
	prunes		
	raisins		

blackberry crumble

4 apples

4 cups (1 lb/500 g) fresh or frozen blackberries or blueberries

2 tsp cornstarch (cornflour)

½ cup (4 oz/125 g) granulated sugar

¾ cup (4 oz/125 g) all-purpose (plain) flour

¾ cup (6 oz/185 g) packed brown sugar

1 cup (3 oz/90 g) old-fashioned rolled oats

½ cup (2 oz/60 g) shredded dried coconut

½ cup (2½ oz/75 g) chopped almonds

2 tsp ground cinnamon

½ tsp ground ginger

½ cup (4 oz/125 g) butter, melted

Preheat oven to 325°F (165°C). Peel, core, and thinly slice apples.

Stir berries, apples, cornstarch, and granulated sugar together in a bowl, then spread in a baking dish 12–14 inches (30–35 cm) in diameter.

Stir flour, brown sugar, oats, coconut, almonds, cinnamon, and ginger together in a bowl. Drizzle with melted butter and toss with a fork to combine. Sprinkle evenly over fruit. Bake until golden and crisp, 45–50 minutes. Serve warm.

Notes: Apples will remain somewhat firm after crumble is baked. If you prefer softer apples, cook them in a covered microwave-proof dish for 7 minutes before mixing with berries. The crumble mixture can be made in bulk to have on hand for quick baked fruit desserts. It will keep in refrigerator for 4 weeks, or can be frozen for longer storage.

To prepare: 20 minutes

To cook: 45–50 minutes

6–8 servings

raisin & cashew truffles

1 cup (6 oz/185 g) raisins

1 cup (6 oz/185 g) dried currants

1 cup (6 oz/185 g) Brazil nuts

1 cup (6 oz/185 g) unsalted roasted cashews

1½ cups (6 oz/185 g) shredded dried coconut

3 Tbsp chopped crystallized ginger

2 Tbsp sweetened condensed milk

Using a food processor or chef's knife, finely chop and blend raisins, currants, Brazil nuts, cashews, 1 cup (4 oz/125 g) coconut, and ginger. Put in a bowl, combine with condensed milk, and stir to blend into a paste. Shape into small balls. Spread remaining ½ cup (2 oz/60 g) coconut on a plate and roll truffles in coconut to coat. Serve at once, or store in an airtight container in refrigerator for up to 4 weeks.

To prepare: 30 minutes

About 50 small truffles

lavender flans

½ cup (4 oz/125 g) plus 3 Tbsp sugar

4 cups (32 fl oz/1 l) low-fat or
whole milk

10 stems organic fresh lavender,
tied in a bunch

5 eggs

1 tsp vanilla extract (essence)

2 or 3 fresh purple plums, pitted and
diced, or ½ cup (2 oz/60 g) fresh
whole blueberries

Preheat oven to 325°F (165°C). Combine ½ cup sugar and 2 Tbsp water in a small saucepan, swirling the pan over medium-high heat until mixture turns a rich amber color, about 9 minutes. While sugar cooks into a caramel, occasionally brush around inner rim of pan with a wet pastry brush to prevent mixture from crystallizing on pan sides. Remove caramel from heat and divide among eight 6– to 8–fl oz (180–250-ml) ramekins or custard cups.

Combine milk with 3 Tbsp sugar and lavender in a saucepan. Bring to a simmer over medium heat, stirring until sugar is dissolved, then remove from heat. Let stand for 15 minutes, then discard lavender.

Lightly whisk eggs and vanilla together in a bowl until just combined (do not overbeat). Stir into warm milk. Strain mixture into prepared ramekins. Place ramekins in a deep baking dish. Pour hot water into dish to come halfway up sides of ramekins. Bake until flans are set, about 35 minutes. Remove from water bath and let cool. Cover and chill for at least 8 hours or up to 2 days to infuse flans with caramel flavor.

Remove flans from refrigerator 30 minutes before serving. Slide a knife around edge to loosen each flan and turn out onto a serving plate. Caramel sauce will pour out onto plates. Scatter diced plums or berries around flans and serve.

To prepare: 20 minutes

To cook: 45–50 minutes,
plus at least 8 hours to chill

8 servings

blueberry coffee cake with crunchy walnut topping

Crunchy Walnut Topping

½ cup (2 oz/60 g) **walnut or pecan pieces**

¼ cup (2 oz/60 g) packed **brown sugar**

2 Tbsp **all-purpose (plain) flour**

1 tsp **ground cinnamon**

2 Tbsp **butter, melted**

Cake

½ cup (4 oz/125 g) **butter, softened**

⅔ cup (5 oz/155 g) **granulated sugar**

1 **egg at room temperature**

1 tsp **vanilla extract (essence)**

½ cup (4 oz/125 g) **low-fat sour cream**

1¾ cups (9 oz/280 g) **all-purpose (plain) flour**

2 tsp **baking powder**

½ tsp **baking soda (bicarbonate of soda)**

1 cup (4 oz/125 g) **fresh or frozen blueberries or raspberries**

Preheat oven to 350°F (180°C). Line bottom of a 9-inch (23-cm) springform pan with parchment (baking) paper.

For Topping: Put walnut pieces in a bowl and sprinkle with brown sugar, flour, and cinnamon. Toss with a fork to combine. Drizzle with melted butter and toss again. Set aside.

For Cake: Cream softened butter and granulated sugar together in a bowl until fluffy. Beat in egg and vanilla. Add sour cream and beat until combined. Sift flour, baking powder, and baking soda together. Add to butter mixture and stir until just combined. Pour batter into prepared pan and smooth top. Sprinkle evenly with berries, then with topping.

Bake until cake is risen, golden in color, and no longer jiggles when pan is shaken, and a wooden skewer inserted in center comes out clean, 55–60 minutes. Remove from oven and let cake stand in pan on a wire rack for 15 minutes before unlatching sides and transferring cake to a plate. Let cool completely, about 2 hours, before slicing.

Note: This cake is best the day it is made but will keep in an airtight container in refrigerator for several days.

To prepare: 20 minutes

To cook: 55–60 minutes, plus 15 minutes to stand and 2 hours to cool

8–10 servings

baked plums
& blackberries

Toss sliced pitted plums and berries with a little vanilla extract (essence) and a sprinkling of sugar and bake at 350°F (180°C) until juicy and soft. Serve with a drizzle of cream or a small scoop of berry sorbet, if desired.

purple grape
& pistachio ricotta

Mix fresh ricotta with grated lemon zest, vanilla extract (essence), and a little allspice or nutmeg. Sweeten with honey. Serve sprinkled with chopped unsalted pistachios and halved purple grapes, or as a spread with crackers and dried figs.

simmered blueberry dessert sauce

For a sauce to accompany ice cream or another dessert, simmer blueberries with 2 Tbsp water and sugar to taste until soft. Mix 1 tsp cornstarch (cornflour) with a little orange juice. Add to simmering fruit and stir until slightly thickened.

frozen blackberry yogurt

Process frozen blackberries or blueberries in a food processor or blender with a squeeze of lemon juice. Add cold yogurt and process again until blended. If desired, sweeten with a little maple syrup. Freeze until ready to serve.

blackberry granita & cream parfait

Granita

1½ cups (12 oz/375 g) granulated sugar

1 cup (4 oz/125 g) fresh or frozen blackberries or boysenberries

¼ cup (2 fl oz/60 ml) lemon juice

Parfait Cream

½ cup (4 fl oz/125 ml) cold heavy (double) cream

¾ cup (6 oz/185 g) plain low-fat or whole yogurt

3 Tbsp powdered (icing) sugar

2 or 3 meringue cookies, crumbled (optional)

Fresh blackberries or boysenberries for garnish (optional)

For Granita: Combine granulated sugar and 3 cups (24 fl oz/750 ml) water in a nonreactive saucepan and cook over medium heat, stirring until sugar is dissolved. Add berries and bring to a boil. Cook for 5 minutes. Remove from heat and stir in lemon juice. With a blender, purée until smooth. Pour into a large, shallow metal baking pan and freeze until icy, about 4 hours. Break up with a fork and freeze 2 hours more. Break up again, then refreeze. About 2 hours before serving, break up mixture again with a fork and refreeze.

For Parfait Cream: In a bowl, whip cream until soft peaks form when the whisk is lifted. Stir in yogurt and powdered sugar. Cover and chill. To serve, spoon alternating layers of granita and parfait cream into serving glasses, sprinkling crumbled meringue, if using, between layers and finishing with a layer of parfait cream. If desired, garnish with fresh berries and serve at once.

Notes: All kinds of acidic fruits can be added to sugar syrup base for granita. Lemon or lime juice works well with a little mint. Store granita in a sealed container in freezer for 4 weeks. Serve without cream if desired.

To cook: 5 minutes

To prepare: 20 minutes, plus at least 8 hours to freeze

6–8 servings

sautéed plums with amaretto

1 Tbsp butter

12 large black plums, halved and pitted

½ cup (4 oz/125 g) sugar

¼ cup (2 fl oz/60 ml) Amaretto liqueur

Greek-Style Yogurt (page 33) for serving

Melt butter in a large frying pan over medium-high heat and cook until starting to brown. Add plums, cut side down, and sprinkle with sugar and Amaretto. Reduce heat to medium-low and cook, shaking pan a couple of times, about 5 minutes. Turn plums and cook 5 minutes more. Turn again and cook until plums start to soften, 3–4 minutes. Do not overcook. Remove to a bowl and let cool. Serve at room temperature, drizzled with liquid from bowl, accompanied with yogurt.

To prepare: 10 minutes

To cook: 17 minutes

5 or 6 servings

Yogurt mousse

100 M /

mango
chèvre
ginger

Fri pm

Sun

dried pineapple
cucumber
onion
? tomato

cucumber
sundried tomatoes
olives
capers   2T

peaches
? triple sec
? Champagne

9:30 nour — shower
— dress
10:40 N

11 am / Mickey

12 home

12:30 Lelde

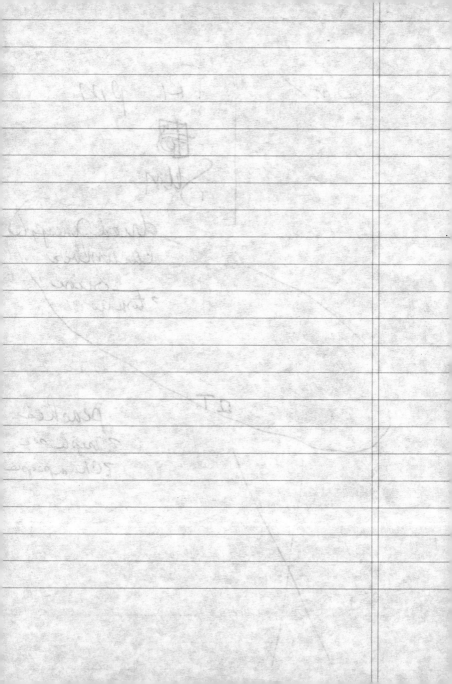

prune compote with greek-style yogurt

Greek-Style Yogurt

1 cup (8 oz/250 g) plain low-fat or whole yogurt

¼ cup (2 oz/60 g) low-fat sour cream

1 lb (500 g) pitted prunes

2 cups (16 fl oz/500 ml) hot black tea

1 cup (8 fl oz/250 ml) red wine or port

1 cup (8 oz/250 g) sugar

½ cup (2½ oz/75 g) blanched almonds (optional)

¼ cup (3 oz/90 g) honey

Juice of 1 lemon

2 or 3 orange zest strips

6 cloves

3 cardamom pods, or 1 tsp cardamom seeds

2-inch (5-cm) cinnamon stick

2–3 Tbsp Cognac or brandy (optional)

Freshly grated nutmeg for garnish

For Greek-Style Yogurt: Line a sieve with cheesecloth (muslin) or a clean thin kitchen towel and set it over a large bowl. Pour in yogurt and let drain for 2–3 hours in refrigerator, until thick. Discard liquid. Pour yogurt into a bowl and mix in sour cream. Refrigerate until ready to use.

Combine all remaining ingredients except Cognac and nutmeg in a saucepan. Bring to a boil, then reduce heat to maintain a simmer. Cook until fruit is plumped and tender, 15 minutes. Remove from heat and stir in Cognac, if using. Let cool, then chill for at least 2 hours.

If you prefer, remove spices and zest strips before serving. Serve prunes with their syrup, garnished with a spoonful of Greek-style yogurt dusted with nutmeg.

Note: *This aromatic compote will keep in refrigerator for up to 2 weeks. It can also be bottled in sterilized jars for longer storage and makes a great Christmas gift. The yogurt will keep for 3–4 days in refrigerator.*

To prepare: 15 minutes, plus 2–3 hours to drain and chill

To cook: 15 minutes

6–8 servings

purple grape tart

1 fully baked 10-inch (25-cm)
Pastry Shell (below)

1 egg white, lightly beaten

3 cups (24 fl oz/750 ml) low-fat or
whole milk

4 egg yolks

½ cup (4 oz/125 g) sugar

2 Tbsp cornstarch (cornflour)

1 Tbsp all-purpose (plain) flour

1 tsp vanilla extract (essence)

Grated zest of ½ lemon

2 Tbsp Cognac or brandy (optional)

¾ lb (375 g) purple grapes

3 Tbsp grape or cranberry jelly

Preheat oven to 350°F (180°C). Brush inside of baked pastry shell with egg white. Bake for 4–5 minutes. Let cool completely.

Heat milk in a saucepan over medium heat to just below a simmer. Whisk egg yolks, sugar, cornstarch, flour, vanilla, lemon zest, and Cognac, if using, together in a bowl until smooth. Whisk a little hot milk into egg mixture, then gradually stir egg mixture into hot milk. Cook over medium heat, stirring constantly, until smooth and thickened, 2–3 minutes. Remove custard filling from heat and let cool for about 1 hour.

Spread custard evenly in cooled pastry shell. Halve and seed grapes and place over custard, cut side down. Chill for at least 20 minutes or up to 6 hours. Just before serving, gently heat jelly, then brush over tart.

Note: Both the pastry shell and the custard filling can be prepared ahead of time, but the tart is best glazed just before serving.

To prepare: 20 minutes

To cook: 15 minutes, plus 1 hour to cool and 20 minutes–6 hours to chill

10 servings

pastry shell

¾ cup (6 oz/185 g) butter, softened

½ cup (3½ oz/105 g) superfine
(caster) sugar

2 eggs, lightly beaten

2–3 Tbsp low-fat or whole milk

2½ cups (12½ oz/390 g) all-purpose
(plain) flour

1 tsp baking powder

⅔ cup (3 oz/90 g) cornstarch
(cornflour)

Canola oil cooking spray

Cream butter and sugar until fluffy. Beat in eggs and milk to blend. Stir in dry ingredients until mixture comes together in a soft ball. Turn out onto a lightly floured work surface and knead lightly. For a 9- or 10-inch (23- or 25-cm) shell, divide into thirds. For tartlets, divide each third into 6 pieces. Press each piece into a disk and wrap in plastic (see Note).

Roll out a dough disk between 2 sheets plastic wrap to form a round 2 inches (5 cm) larger in diameter than tart pan. Remove plastic from the top and carefully invert dough into a tart pan. Press dough firmly and evenly into pan, ensuring that sides are not too thick. Remove plastic and run rolling pin over top to trim. Chill for 10–15 minutes.

Preheat oven to 325°F (165°C). Cover dough with oiled parchment (baking) paper or foil. Press evenly into corners of dough and fill with pie weights or dried beans. For a partially baked shell, bake for 15 minutes. If paper sticks to pastry, bake for a few more minutes; it should come off easily. Remove paper and weights. For a fully baked shell, after removing paper and weights, bake until a pale golden color, 15–20 minutes more.

Note: This recipe makes dough for multiple tarts, which you can refrigerate for up to 1 week or freeze for up to 6 months.

To prepare: 30 minutes, plus 10 minutes to chill

To cook: about 30 minutes

Three 9-inch (23-cm) or 10-inch (25-cm) pastry shells or eighteen 4½-inch (11.5-cm) pastry shells

honeydew melons green pears

GREEN FRUITS AND VEGETABLES BOOST THE IMMUNE

fresh mint avocados key limes

SYSTEM • PROMOTE EYE HEALTH • HELP BUILD STRONG

green apples kiwifruits persian

BONES • BUILD STRONG TEETH • OFFER ANTIOXIDANTS

limes green grapes fresh basil

FOR HEALING AND PROTECTION • REDUCE THE RISK OF

honeydew melons green pears

CERTAIN CANCERS • GREEN FRUITS AND VEGETABLES

fresh mint avocados key limes

BOOST THE IMMUNE SYSTEM • PROMOTE EYE HEALTH

Green

Green is the color of growing things. The flavor of green fruits is light, fresh, and clean, and their texture is crisp and juicy. They are naturally good for you, and since so many fruits are green, you'll find a good variety available year-round, not just a brief summertime explosion. And green tea and green herbs both share the antioxidant benefits of green fruits, and make interesting additions to a dessert.

In the heat of midsummer, green fruits like honeydew melon and green grapes make cool and refreshing finishes to a light supper. Frozen grapes (see Green Tea Punch, page 41) make a simple and fun dessert or snack on their own. Or turn to page 47 for a very easy salad that pairs juicy green melon with luscious avocado.

The appearance of apples and pears at farmers' markets is a sure sign that autumn is arriving, the weather is turning cool, and it's time to start baking. A spiced apple cake is a classic holiday-time dessert (page 41). Pears are so elegant that even simply baking them with a spice-and-nut filling makes an impressive finale to a meal (page 45).

The winter months bring tropical kiwifruits and bright, cheery citrus fruits such as lemons and limes. You can combine the complementary flavors of both in a pretty tart or tartlet (page 48). Kiwifruit Sorbet (page 42), sparked with lemon juice, offers a light and fresh alternative to the usual rich ice cream flavors.

SPRING	SUMMER	AUTUMN	WINTER
green apples	green apples	green apples	green apples
avocados	avocados	green grapes	avocados
green grapes	green grapes	herbs	green grapes
herbs	herbs	kiwifruits	kiwifruits
kiwifruits	green pears	Persian limes	Persian limes
Persian and Key limes	Persian and Key limes	green-fleshed melons	green pears
green-fleshed melons	green melons	green pears	green tea
green pears	green tea	green tea	
green tea			

spiced apple cake

3 green apples

1 cup (8 oz/250 g) granulated sugar

½ cup (4 oz/125 g) butter, melted

1 egg

1¼ cups (6½ oz/200 g) all-purpose (plain) flour

1 tsp baking soda (bicarbonate of soda)

1 tsp ground cinnamon

½ tsp freshly grated nutmeg

½ tsp ground allspice

½ tsp salt

½ cup (3 oz/90 g) golden raisins (sultanas)

2 Tbsp granulated sugar mixed with 1 tsp ground cinnamon

Powdered (icing) sugar for dusting

Preheat oven to 325°F (165°C). Butter an 8-inch (20-cm) round cake pan. Core and thinly slice apples, leaving skin intact. Whisk granulated sugar, butter, and egg together in a bowl. Stir in two-thirds of the apple slices.

Sift flour, baking soda, cinnamon, nutmeg, allspice, and salt together. Add to egg mixture along with raisins, stirring until just blended. Pour into prepared pan and smooth top. Arrange remaining apple slices in a pattern on top, pressing them gently into batter. Sprinkle with cinnamon sugar. Bake until golden and springy to touch, about 50 minutes. Let cake stand in pan on a wire rack for 10 minutes, then turn out and let cool completely, about 2 hours. Dust with powdered sugar and cut into wedges to serve.

Notes: You can use any type of apples in season. The cake will taste slightly different every time but is always moist, as well as easy to prepare. Store cake in a covered container in refrigerator for up to 4 days.

To prepare: 20 minutes

To cook: 50 minutes, plus 10 minutes to stand and 2 hours to cool

8–10 servings

green tea punch

3 cups (18 oz/560 g) seedless green grapes

4 tsp best-quality green tea leaves, or 6 green tea bags

2 Tbsp sugar

1 cup (8 fl oz/250 ml) pineapple juice

1 cup (8 fl oz/250 ml) ginger beer or ginger ale

2 Tbsp lime juice

Put grapes on a baking sheet and freeze for at least 2 hours. (To freeze longer, transfer to a covered container.) Bring 6 cups (48 fl oz/1.5 l) water to a boil, let stand for 1 minute, then pour over tea leaves and sugar in a teapot. Let stand for 2–3 minutes. Strain into a bowl, let cool, and chill.

To serve, stir pineapple juice, ginger beer, and lime juice into cold tea. Pour into a pitcher or serving glasses and add frozen grapes.

To prepare: 10 minutes, plus 2 hours to chill and freeze

6–8 servings

kiwifruit sorbet

6 kiwifruits, peeled

⅔ cup (5 oz/155 g) sugar

½ cup (4 fl oz/125 ml) lemon juice

12 fresh mint leaves, thinly sliced

1 egg white

3 Tbsp Cointreau or other liqueur
of choice (optional)

Garnish
Lemon zest strips
Sliced peeled kiwifruits

Purée kiwifruits in a blender just until smooth. Do not overblend, or seeds will break up and make purée bitter. Measure out 2 cups (16 fl oz/ 500 ml) purée. Set aside.

Combine sugar and 1½ cups (12 fl oz/375 ml) water in a saucepan and bring to a boil over medium heat, stirring to dissolve sugar. Simmer syrup for 5 minutes. Let cool and chill for 2 hours.

In a bowl, mix kiwi purée with lemon juice, mint, and cold syrup. Pour into a shallow metal baking pan and freeze until icy, about 4 hours. Process in a food processor or beat with an electric mixer until smooth. Add egg white and liqueur, if using, and process or beat until fluffy. Refreeze until firm, about 4 hours, then beat again. Pack sorbet into a container and freeze completely, 4 hours more. Serve in chilled glasses, garnished with lemon zest and sliced kiwifruits.

To prepare: 30 minutes, plus 2 hours to chill and 12 hours to freeze

To cook: 5 minutes

6–8 servings

silky lime mousse

⅔ cup (5 oz/155 g) low-fat or whole plain yogurt

3 eggs, separated

Finely grated zest of 3 limes

4–6 Tbsp lime juice (about 4 limes)

⅓ cup (2½ oz/75 g) superfine (caster) sugar

1½ tsp unflavored powdered gelatin

⅔ cup (5 fl oz/160 ml) cold heavy (double) cream

Line a sieve with cheesecloth (muslin) or a clean thin kitchen towel and set it over a large bowl. Pour in yogurt and let drain for 2–3 hours in refrigerator, until thick. Discard liquid.

Combine yolks, lime zest and juice, and half of sugar in a large heatproof bowl and set over a saucepan with 2 inches (5 cm) of simmering water. Whisk constantly until yolks are pale and thickened. Remove bowl from pan and set aside.

Sprinkle gelatin over ¼ cup (2 fl oz/60 ml) cold water and let stand until absorbed, about 3 minutes. Heat in a microwave for 30–40 seconds or in a pan on the stove top for 1–2 minutes to dissolve. Stir to ensure that gelatin is fully dissolved. Whisk into lime mixture. Chill until mixture starts to set, about 40 minutes.

In a bowl, whip cream until soft peaks form when the whisk is lifted and fold into lime mixture. Fold in yogurt. In a large bowl, beat egg whites until foamy, then gradually beat in remaining sugar until soft peaks form. Fold lime mixture into beaten whites. Spoon into individual dishes or a large serving dish. Chill until set, about 3 hours, then serve.

To prepare: 20 minutes, plus 3 hours to drain yogurt and 3¾ hours to set mousse

To cook: 5 minutes

6 servings

baked apples with caramel sauce

6 large green-skinned apples such as Granny Smith

½ cup (2 oz/60 g) dried cranberries or cherries

¼ cup (1 oz/30 g) pecans or walnuts, chopped

½ tsp ground cinnamon

½ tsp ground allspice

¼ tsp freshly grated nutmeg

Caramel Sauce
1 cup (8 oz/250 g) sugar

½ cup (5½ oz/170 g) light corn syrup

1 Tbsp lemon juice

2 Tbsp butter

Preheat oven to 350°F (180°C). Using an apple corer, cut out cores from apples in neat plugs. Use a paring knife to enlarge each cavity to 1 inch (2.5 cm) in diameter. Cut off a thin ring of peel around circumference of each apple with knife. Place apples in a shallow baking dish. Stir cranberries, nuts, and spices together in a bowl. Divide mixture evenly among apples, stuffing into cavities.

For Caramel Sauce: Combine sugar, 3 Tbsp water, corn syrup, and lemon juice in a saucepan and bring to a boil over medium heat. Cook until sauce turns a rich amber color, about 15 minutes, brushing inside of pan with a wet pastry brush to prevent mixture from crystallizing. Remove from heat and stir in butter until smooth.

Pour hot sauce over apples. Bake until apples are wrinkly and soft, 30–35 minutes. Serve hot, topped with caramel sauce.

To prepare: 30 minutes

To cook: 45–60 minutes

6 servings

stuffed green pears

4 green-skinned pears, stems intact

½ cup (2½ oz/75 g) almonds, chopped

½ cup (2½ oz/75 g) ground almonds

2 Tbsp packed brown sugar

Grated zest of ½ lemon

1 tsp ground cloves

1 egg white

½ cup (5½ oz/170 g) maple syrup

Preheat oven to 325°F (165°C). Using an apple corer or teaspoon, cut out cores from bottom of pears (leaving a little of the core at the top will help keep stem attached). Use a teaspoon to enlarge each cavity enough to hold 2 Tbsp filling.

Stir chopped almonds, ground almonds, sugar, lemon zest, cloves, and egg white together in a small bowl. Divide mixture evenly among pears, pressing firmly into cavities. Stand pears in a shallow baking dish (if necessary, cut slices from the bottoms so they stand upright). Drizzle with maple syrup. Cover tightly with foil and bake until pears are easily pierced with a skewer, about 1 hour. To serve, place pears on plates and spoon syrup on top.

To prepare: 15 minutes

To cook: 1 hour

4 servings

melon in spiced syrup

Combine equal amounts of sugar and water in a pan and stir over medium heat until sugar dissolves. Add grated ginger, star anise, and lemon zest and juice and simmer gently for 10 minutes. Cool, strain, and serve over sliced honeydew.

kiwifruit sandwiches

Spread thin, crisp cookies such as brandy snaps with apricot jam. Layer with sliced kiwifruit and top with ricotta cheese flavored with a little lemon juice, honey, and cinnamon.

baked fruit parcels

Place grape, pear, and kiwi slices or
chunks on parchment paper. Drizzle with
honey, scatter with minced ginger, add
whole spices such as cardamom, star
anise, or cinnamon, and enclose. Bake
at 350°F (180°C) for about 30 minutes.

avocado & melon salad

Combine chunks of just-ripe avocado
and green-fleshed melon and spoon into
serving glasses over thick Greek-Style
Yogurt (page 33). Drizzle with honey and
plenty of lime or lemon juice.

kiwifruit tart with lime curd filling

Lime Curd

1 cup (8 oz/250 g) sugar

¾ cup (6 oz/185 g) plus 2 Tbsp butter, diced

Grated zest of 3 limes

½ cup (4 fl oz/125 ml) lime juice

4 eggs, lightly beaten

1 fully baked 10-inch (25-cm) Pastry Shell or 6 individual Pastry Shells (page 34)

1 egg white, lightly beaten

4 or 5 kiwifruits, peeled and thinly sliced

3 Tbsp apricot jam or passion fruit syrup

For Lime Curd: Combine sugar, butter, and lime zest and juice in a saucepan and bring to a boil over medium heat, stirring to dissolve sugar. Remove from heat, whisk in eggs, and pour into a heatproof bowl. Set over a saucepan with 2 inches (5 cm) of simmering water. Stir constantly until mixture is thick enough to coat the back of a spoon, 6–8 minutes. (If you have a candy thermometer, you can cook mixture directly over low heat. Stir constantly just until it reaches 170°F/77°C. Remove from heat and stir for a minute.) Let cool, cover surface with parchment (baking) paper to prevent a skin from forming, and chill until ready to use.

Preheat oven to 350°F (180°C). Brush inside of baked pastry shell with egg white. Bake for 4–5 minutes to set egg white. Let cool completely on a wire rack.

Spoon chilled lime curd into cooled pastry shell and arrange sliced kiwifruits on top. Gently heat jam and strain to remove any solids. Brush over tart to glaze. Serve at once.

Notes: The tart(s) can be assembled without glaze up to 8 hours ahead. Brush with glaze just before serving. The curd keeps well in a covered container in refrigerator for up to 10 days. It can also be bottled in sterilized jars for longer storage and gift giving.

To prepare: 15 minutes

To cook: 5 minutes

8 servings

minted green tea jellies with kiwifruit

4 tsp unflavored powdered gelatin

¼ cup (2 oz/60 g) sugar

1 tsp green tea powder

12 fresh mint leaves

2 kiwifruits, peeled and finely diced

Juice of 1 lime

In a cup, sprinkle gelatin over 2 Tbsp cold water and let stand until absorbed, about 3 minutes. Heat in a microwave for 20 seconds or in a small saucepan over low heat on the stove top for about 1 minute to dissolve. Stir to ensure that gelatin is fully dissolved.

In a large bowl, combine sugar and green tea powder. Stir in 2 Tbsp water to form a paste.

In a saucepan, bring 2 cups (16 fl oz/500 ml) water to a boil and pour over mint in a heatproof bowl. Let stand for 2 minutes, then strain and add mint-flavored water to tea paste along with gelatin mixture. Discard mint. Stir until sugar is completely dissolved.

Divide mixture among four ½-cup (4–fl oz/125-ml) serving glasses or bowls. Chill until set, about 5 hours, stirring several times before mixture sets to prevent separating. Just before serving, garnish with dice kiwifruits and drizzle with a little fresh lime juice.

Notes: These jellies are set very softly. If you prefer a firmer set, increase gelatin. Kiwifruits contain an enzyme that prevents setting, so don't garnish jellies until ready to serve, or they will break down.

To prepare: 20 minutes, plus at least 5 hours to chill

4 servings

ginger white peaches tan pears

WHITE AND TAN FRUITS AND VEGETABLES CONTAIN

bananas dates white nectarines

ANTIOXIDANTS FOR HEALING AND PROTECTION • HELP

dried white peaches white corn

MAINTAIN A HEALTHY CHOLESTEROL LEVEL • PROMOTE

ginger tan figs white peaches

HEART HEALTH • BOOST THE IMMUNE SYSTEM • SLOW

tan pears bananas dates white

CHOLESTEROL ABSORPTION • WHITE AND TAN FRUITS

nectarines dried white peaches

AND VEGETABLES OFFER ANTIOXIDANTS FOR HEALING

White & tan

Eating a healthy diet means eating a wide variety of foods, constantly changing your body's sources of energy and nutrients to get the broadest range possible. White foods like refined sugar and flour may be less than desirable, but white and tan fruits offer an array of coveted benefits. If you include the dried forms, some fruits in this color group are available year-round.

Bananas are white—at least the part you eat—and are a most versatile fruit. They make a good addition to breakfast cereal and a convenient self-contained snack anytime of day. But don't overlook them as a dessert ingredient. They give baked goods such as Streusel Banana Muffins (page 68) an appealing moistness and provide nutritious substance for an updated banana split with Asian flavors (page 62).

Considered a tan food, fresh ginger is valued as a traditional medicine for its stomach-settling properties. These effects make ginger a good counterbalance to a rich dinner, so it has long been a favorite ingredient in desserts. Here, the warm, spicy flavor of gingerbread is intensified by using two forms of ginger in one recipe (page 61): ground and crystallized.

In summer, you'll want to make the most of juicy fresh peaches and nectarines while they last, in a rustic tart (page 67) or by brushing the fruits with honey and roasting them (page 63).

SPRING	SUMMER	AUTUMN	WINTER
bananas	bananas	bananas	dates
dried tan figs	white corn	dates	dried tan figs
ginger	tan figs	tan figs	ginger
dried white nectarines	white nectarines	ginger	dried white nectarines
dried white peaches	white peaches	dried white nectarines	dried white peaches
tan-skinned pears		dried white peaches	tan pears
		tan pears	

ginger angel food cakes

½ cup (2 oz/60 g) cake (soft-wheat) flour

½ tsp baking powder

¾ cup (5 oz/150 g) superfine (caster) sugar

6 large egg whites

¾ tsp cream of tartar

Pinch of salt

1 Tbsp finely grated fresh ginger

1 tsp vanilla extract (essence)

Grated zest of ½ lemon

Ginger Icing

1 cup (4 oz/125 g) powdered (icing) sugar

1 Tbsp lemon juice

1 Tbsp minced ginger in syrup or crystallized ginger (see Notes)

1 Tbsp syrup from ginger in syrup or water

Preheat oven to 350°F (180°C). Sift flour, baking powder, and ½ cup (3 oz/90 g) superfine sugar together 3 times.

In a large bowl, beat egg whites with cream of tartar and salt until soft peaks form when the whisk is lifted. Add ginger, vanilla, and lemon zest. Gradually beat in remaining ¼ cup (2 oz/60 g) sugar until dissolved. Using a large slotted spoon, gently fold in dry ingredients just until evenly blended.

Spoon batter into 6 nonstick large muffin cups or 10 standard muffin cups. Bake until cakes are springy to the touch, 25–30 minutes.

For Icing: In a bowl, combine powdered sugar and lemon juice. Stir in minced ginger and ginger syrup to form a runny icing.

Remove cakes from oven, invert onto a wire rack, and let cool completely. Lift off pan. Spoon a little icing over each cake, and serve.

Notes: Ginger in syrup is available in Asian markets and some specialty food shops, or by mail order online. If you can't find ginger in syrup, use water and a little chopped crystallized ginger instead. Garnish cakes with chopped crystallized ginger if desired. Store cakes in an airtight container for up to 3 days.

To prepare: 20 minutes

To cook: 25–30 minutes

6 or 10 individual cakes

caramelized bananas

3 Tbsp butter

¼ cup (2 oz/60 g) packed brown sugar

1 cup (8 fl oz/250 ml) apple or pineapple juice

2 Tbsp lime juice

6–8 small finger bananas or 3 or 4 regular bananas, peeled and halved lengthwise

Vanilla frozen yogurt for serving

Melt butter in a frying pan over medium heat and cook until it bubbles and starts to brown. Add sugar, apple juice, and lime juice. Cook over medium-high heat until syrupy, 8–10 minutes. Reduce heat to medium, add bananas, and cook until slightly softened, 3–4 minutes, turning gently with tongs to cook both sides. Serve bananas with their sauce, accompanied with vanilla frozen yogurt.

To prepare: 15 minutes

To cook: 15 minutes

3 or 4 servings

sauternes-poached pears

4–6 firm tan-skinned pears, stems intact

1 bottle (24 fl oz/750 ml) Sauternes or other dessert wine

½ cup (4 oz/125 g) sugar

1 cinnamon stick

2 bay leaves

Choose a pot that will hold pears fairly snugly when fruits stand upright. Set pears aside and heat Sauternes and sugar in pot over medium heat, stirring until sugar is dissolved. Add pears, cinnamon, and bay leaves, arranging pears so they are submerged as much as possible in syrup. Cover pears with a circle of parchment (baking) paper a bit larger than pot to help keep them moist.

Return liquid to a simmer, then reduce heat to low, cover, and cook pears very gently until tender, about 40 minutes, turning several times so they cook evenly. Carefully lift pears from syrup with a slotted spoon. Raise heat to high and boil syrup to reduce it a little and concentrate flavors, about 5 minutes. Serve pears warm or cold with a little syrup.

Notes: Pears can be cooked, covered, and refrigerated for up to 4 days in syrup (this actually improves their flavor). If you prefer pears served warm, reheat gently in the syrup. Leftover syrup can be used to cook more pears or stone fruits.

To prepare: 5 minutes

To cook: 45 minutes

4–6 servings

crystallized-ginger gingerbread

4 Tbsp (2 oz/60 g) butter, softened

½ cup (4 oz/125 g) granulated sugar

½ cup (5½ oz/170 g) molasses

½ cup (3 oz/90 g) minced crystallized ginger

2 eggs at room temperature

1½ cups (7½ oz/235 g) all-purpose (plain) flour

1 tsp baking soda (bicarbonate of soda)

2 tsp ground ginger

½ tsp ground cinnamon

½ tsp ground allspice

¼ tsp freshly grated nutmeg

½ cup (4 fl oz/125 ml) buttermilk or plain low-fat or whole yogurt

Demerara or other raw sugar for sprinkling (optional)

Preheat oven to 350°F (180°C). Butter a 9 x 4–inch (23 x 10–cm) loaf pan and line bottom with parchment (baking) paper.

Cream butter and granulated sugar together in a bowl until fluffy. Stir in molasses and minced ginger. Beat in eggs one at a time. Sift dry ingredients together. Stir into butter mixture in 3 additions alternately with buttermilk in 2 additions, mixing until smooth.

Pour into prepared pan and smooth top. Bake until gingerbread is golden and springy to the touch and a skewer inserted in center comes out clean, 45–50 minutes. Let gingerbread stand in pan on a wire rack for 10 minutes. Turn out and serve warm or at room temperature, sprinkled with demerara sugar, if using.

Notes: This tender, moist, dark gingerbread is good served warm with poached pears and their syrup (page 58) or a bowl of Greek-style yogurt (page 33). Or, try it with afternoon tea or coffee. Store in an airtight container for up to 1 week.

To prepare: 10 minutes

To cook: 45–50 minutes

1 large loaf, 10–12 servings

white nectarines with lychees & grapes

4 perfectly ripe white nectarines

2 cups (12 oz/375 g) seedless green grapes

1 can (18 oz/560 g) lychees in juice

1 Tbsp lime juice

Halve, pit, and thinly slice nectarines. Halve grapes. Drain lychees, reserving juice, and finely dice.

Pour reserved lychee juice into a serving bowl. Add prepared fruit to bowl, sprinkle with lime juice, and mix gently to combine.

Chill for at least 1 hour or up to 4 hours before serving.

To prepare: 15 minutes, plus 1 hour to chill

6 servings

labne with ginger, grapes & almonds

Drain yogurt overnight in a lined sieve (see page 33) to produce soft labne cheese. Mix with powdered (icing) sugar and lemon juice to taste. Serve with chopped crystallized ginger, grapes, toasted almonds, and sliced tan pears.

banana-coconut split

Update a classic banana split with sliced bananas, peeled or canned lychees, a scoop of coconut ice cream, and a drizzle of purchased or homemade passion fruit or mango sauce. Garnish with toasted dried shredded coconut.

roasted white nectarines

Halve and pit white nectarines and brush with honey or sprinkle with brown sugar. Roast in a hot oven or on grill until browned and caramelized. Serve with a garnish of cream or crème fraîche and thyme or lavender, if desired.

kaffir-infused pears

Kaffir lime leaves have a tropical flavor that complements fruit well. Toss finely shredded Kaffir lime leaves and mint leaves with sliced tan-skinned pears such as Bosc and/or Asian pears. Stir in a little lime juice and sugar to taste.

fresh dates with pistachio-mascarpone filling

Pistachio-Mascarpone Filling

½ cup (3 oz/90 g) raisins

½ cup (3 oz/90 g) dried figs

¼ cup (1 oz/30 g) pistachio nuts

¼ cup (1½ oz/45 g) dried apricots

2 Tbsp finely chopped crystallized ginger

½ cup (4 oz/125 g) mascarpone cheese

Grated zest of ½ lemon

½ tsp ground cardamom

25 fresh dates or figs

For Filling: Finely chop raisins, dried figs, pistachios, and apricots. Combine in a bowl with ginger, mascarpone, lemon zest, and cardamom and stir to blend.

Split dates along one side and remove pits, or cut a notch in top of each fresh fig. Fill each date or fig with 1 tsp filling. Serve at once, or refrigerate until ready to serve.

Note: Filled dates and figs will keep in a covered container in refrigerator for up to 3 days.

To prepare: 20 minutes

4 servings

brandied baked figs

12–14 large tan-skinned figs

½ lemon, very thinly sliced (unpeeled)

½-inch (12-mm) piece fresh ginger, peeled and very thinly sliced

⅓ cup (3 oz/90 g) sugar

½ cup (4 fl oz/125 ml) brandy

Crème fraîche or mascarpone for serving (optional)

Preheat oven to 300°F (150°C). Arrange the figs in a baking dish that holds them fairly snugly. Scatter lemon and ginger slices on top. Sprinkle with sugar and drizzle with brandy. Wrap dish tightly with foil and bake until figs are very tender, about 1½ hours, turning once after 1 hour. Let cool on a wire rack, then chill for at least 2 hours before serving. Accompany figs with their brandied cooking syrup and crème fraîche, if using.

Note: Store figs in their syrup in refrigerator for up to 1 week.

To prepare: 10 minutes

To cook: 1½ hours, plus 2 hours to chill

4–6 servings

white peach crostatas

½ recipe Cornmeal Pastry (page 79)

2 large or 3 medium white peaches, halved, pitted, and very thinly sliced (about 20 slices per peach)

2 Tbsp lemon juice

¼ cup (2 oz/60 g) granulated sugar

1 Tbsp powdered (icing) sugar for dusting

Preheat oven to 400°F (200°C). Roll out pastry on a lightly floured work surface to ⅛ inch (3 mm) thick. Cut into six 6-inch (15-cm) rounds, rerolling pastry as needed. Place rounds on a baking sheet, allowing a little space between them. Fan peach slices in a ring in center of each round, leaving a ½-inch (12-mm) margin around edge. Fold in edge to slightly enclose peaches, crimping gently with your fingers to hold pastry together where it overlaps. Brush peaches with lemon juice and sprinkle with granulated sugar. Bake until golden, about 35 minutes. Serve warm or at room temperature, dusted with powdered sugar.

Note: Don't worry if peaches turn brown as they are being prepared; they will brown further during cooking as the sugar caramelizes. These crostatas are best eaten the day they are made.

To prepare: 20 minutes, plus 40 minutes for pastry

To cook: 35 minutes

6 servings

sweet corn bread

2 cups (10 oz/315 g) all-purpose (plain) flour

1 cup (7 oz/220 g) instant polenta

½ cup (4 oz/125 g) sugar

2 tsp baking powder

1 tsp baking soda (bicarbonate of soda)

½ tsp salt

1 cup (8 fl oz/250 ml) buttermilk

2 Tbsp maple syrup

2 eggs

½ cup (4 fl oz/125 ml) canola oil

2 ripe bananas, mashed

½ cup (3 oz/90 g) white corn kernels

Butter a 9 x 5–inch (23 x 13–cm) loaf pan and line bottom with parchment (baking) paper. Preheat oven to 350°F (180°C). Stir flour, polenta, sugar, baking powder, baking soda, and salt together in a bowl until blended. Whisk buttermilk, maple syrup, eggs, and oil together in another bowl. Stir in bananas, then add to dry ingredients with corn kernels and stir until just combined (do not overmix). Pour into prepared pan and smooth top. Bake until loaf is risen and firm to the touch and a skewer inserted in center comes out clean, about 50 minutes. Let corn bread stand in pan on a wire rack for 15 minutes, then turn out onto rack to cool completely, about 1 hour. Slice and serve.

Note: This corn bread makes great brunch fare, toasted and topped with maple syrup and crisp bacon.

To prepare: 15 minutes

To cook: 50 minutes, plus 15 minutes to stand and 1 hour to cool

6–8 servings

streusel banana muffins

Streusel Topping

⅓ cup (2 oz/60 g) all-purpose (plain) flour

¼ cup (2 oz/60 g) packed brown sugar

4 Tbsp (2 oz/60 g) butter, melted

¼ cup (1 oz/30 g) chopped almonds

2 cups (10 oz/315 g) all-purpose (plain) flour

1½ cups (3¾ oz/115 g) bran flakes or wheat bran

3 tsp baking powder

3 tsp ground cinnamon

1 tsp ground ginger

1 cup (8 fl oz/250 ml) low-fat or whole milk

3 Tbsp butter

3 Tbsp light corn syrup

½ cup (3½ oz/105 g) packed brown sugar

1 tsp baking soda (bicarbonate of soda)

2 ripe large bananas, mashed

Preheat oven to 400°F (200°C). Butter 12 standard muffin cups, or line with paper liners.

For Streusel Topping: In a bowl, combine flour and sugar and toss with a fork to blend. Drizzle 4 Tbsp melted butter over and stir in almonds. Set aside.

Stir flour, bran, baking powder, cinnamon, and ginger together in a large bowl and stir with a fork to blend.

Combine milk, butter, corn syrup, and sugar in a microwave-proof bowl and heat in microwave or in a saucepan over medium heat on stove top until butter is melted and sugar is dissolved, about 2 minutes in microwave or 4–5 minutes on stove. Stir in baking soda and mashed bananas. Add wet ingredients to dry ingredients and mix until just combined. Do not overmix.

Spoon batter into prepared muffin cups. Sprinkle with streusel topping. Bake until muffins are risen and golden, 15–20 minutes. Let muffins stand in pan on a wire rack for 2–3 minutes, then turn out and serve.

Notes: *If you have overripe bananas, this is one of the best ways to use them. Make a batch of muffin mixture, store it in the refrigerator, and bake a few muffins at a time so that you can enjoy fresh muffins throughout the week with very little effort. The baked muffins also freeze well.*

To prepare: 15 minutes

To cook: 15–20 minutes

12 muffins

apricots yellow apples mangoes

YELLOW AND ORANGE FRUITS AND VEGETABLES HELP

grapefruit peaches pineapples

PROMOTE HEART HEALTH • HELP REDUCE THE RISK OF

yellow gooseberries nectarines

CERTAIN CANCERS • PROMOTE EYE HEALTH • CONTAIN

pumpkins oranges persimmons

ANTIOXIDANTS FOR HEALING AND PROTECTION • BOOST

carrots sweet potatoes lemons

THE IMMUNE SYSTEM • YELLOW AND ORANGE FRUITS

golden kiwifruits dried apricots

AND VEGETABLES OFFER ANTIOXIDANTS FOR HEALING

Yellow & orange

Nutritionists have long known that yellow and orange fruits and vegetables are excellent sources of the antioxidant beta-carotene, which the body converts into essential vitamin A, but only recently have the full benefits of this color group of produce come to light. Orange fruits and vegetables taste bright and zesty, and they help keep us healthy in many ways throughout the year.

Orange and yellow citrus fruits make several appearances in this chapter, and not only in the most common forms. For a change of pace, try tiny kumquats preserved in brandy (page 81) or a simple ice cream made from the mild Meyer lemon, a hybrid of lemon and mandarin orange (page 75). Many citrus fruits come into season in autumn and winter, offering the cold-fighting benefits of vitimin C just when we most need them.

The yellow stone fruits of summer—peaches, nectarines, and apricots—are a fleeting pleasure. Enjoy them during their brief season as part of a simple tart (page 79) or an even simpler dessert of poached fruit with a tart raspberry sauce (page 80).

Orange vegetables are among the handful that play regular roles in baked desserts. Carrots make moist and sweet cupcakes (page 82). Sweet potatoes contribute generous doses of vitamins A, C, and E to your diet, as well as antioxidants. Enjoy these benefits in a sweet potato pie (page 86) with a wholesome graham cracker crust.

SPRING	SUMMER	AUTUMN	WINTER
yellow apples	apricots	yellow apples	yellow apples
apricots	dried apricots	dried apricots	dried apricots
dried apricots	carrots	carrots	carrots
carrots	corn	golden kiwifruits	grapefruits
corn	yellow gooseberries	lemons	golden kiwifruits
grapefruits	lemons	yellow- & orange-fleshed melons	kumquats
golden kiwifruits	mangoes	navel & mandarin oranges	lemons
kumquat	yellow- & orange-fleshed melons	papayas	navel & mandarin oranges
lemons	nectarines	yellow pears	yellow pears
mangoes	Valencia oranges	persimmons	pumpkins
navel & mandarin oranges	peaches	pumpkins	sweet potatoes
papayas	golden raspberries	sweet potatoes	
pineapples			

meyer lemon meringue ice cream

1½ cups (10½ oz/330 g) superfine (caster) sugar

Grated zest of 1 Meyer lemon

½–⅔ cup (4–5 fl oz/125–160 ml) Meyer lemon juice, strained (see Notes)

4 egg whites

1 cup (8 fl oz/250 ml) heavy (double) cream

Combine sugar, lemon zest, and lemon juice in a small saucepan. Cook over low heat, stirring, until sugar is dissolved. Raise heat to medium-high and cook until mixture reaches consistency of a thick syrup and large bubbles form as it boils, about 5 minutes. Mixture is ready when it reaches 225°F (110°C) on a candy thermometer.

With an electric mixer on medium speed, beat egg whites until stiff, glossy peaks form when whisk is lifted. On low speed, gradually add hot syrup and beat until cool and very thick, about 10 minutes.

In a deep bowl, beat cream until soft peaks form. Using a large, flat spoon, fold into egg white mixture until evenly blended. Place in a freezer-proof container, cover, and freeze until firm, about 4 hours.

Notes: An ice-cream maker is not needed to produce this creamy, smooth ice cream. For a tarter flavor, use larger quantity of lemon juice. Or, use regular lemon instead of milder Meyer, but reduce juice quantity to ½ cup (4 fl oz/125 ml) and increase sugar to 1¾ cups (12½ oz/390 g). Two or three Tbsp limoncello or other lemon liqueur may be added to the whipped cream; it will make the ice cream slightly softer. Store in freezer for up to 4 weeks.

To prepare: 40 minutes

To cook: 5 minutes, plus at least 4 hours to freeze

1½ quarts, 6 servings

orange & sabayon gratin

2 egg yolks

⅓ cup (3 oz/90 g) sugar

¾ cup (6 fl oz/180 ml) Muscat or other late-harvest dessert wine, or sparkling wine

2 Tbsp heavy (double) cream

5 oranges, peeled and segmented

Whisk egg yolks and sugar together in a heatproof bowl until very pale and thick. Whisk in wine. Set bowl over a saucepan with 2 inches (5 cm) of simmering water. Whisk constantly until mixture is thick enough to coat the back of a spoon, about 5 minutes. Transfer bowl to a larger bowl of ice water to stop cooking. Whisk in cream. Use at once, or cover and chill.

To serve, preheat a broiler (grill). Divide orange segments among 4 individual gratin dishes. Whisk sabayon and pour over fruit. Broil (grill) just until sabayon starts to turn golden, 2–3 minutes.

Note: Sabayon will keep, refrigerated, for up to 24 hours.

To prepare: 25 minutes

To cook: 2–3 minutes

4 servings

papaya & mango tapioca

½ cup (3 oz/90 g) small pearl tapioca

¼ cup (2 fl oz/60 ml) unsweetened coconut cream

2 Tbsp granulated sugar

1 large mango, peeled and diced

½ medium or large papaya, peeled, seeded, and sliced

Juice of 1 lime

4 tsp demerara or other raw sugar, or grated palm sugar

Bring 4 cups (32 fl oz/1 l) water to a boil over high heat. Reduce heat to a simmer, add tapioca, and cook until translucent, 12–15 minutes. Drain thoroughly through a fine-mesh sieve. Put in a bowl and stir in coconut cream and granulated sugar, stirring to dissolve sugar. Cover and chill for at least 1 hour or up to 24 hours.

Divide among individual serving bowls and top with fruit. Drizzle with lime juice and sprinkle with demerara sugar.

Note: Uncooked pearl tapioca can be found at Asian markets and natural foods stores. This is quite a rich dessert, so the servings are small.

To prepare: 20 minutes

To cook: 15 minutes, plus 1 hour to chill

4 servings

honey-glazed pineapple

1 large pineapple

⅓ cup (4 oz/125 g) honey

6 star anise

Lime wedges for garnish

Cut peel from pineapple, trim away eyes, and halve lengthwise. Remove core from pineapple halves and cut each half crosswise into 8–10 slices 1 inch (2.5 cm) thick. Put in a shallow baking dish, drizzle with honey, and scatter with star anise. Let stand at room temperature to macerate for at least 30 minutes or refrigerate for up to 4 hours. Turn pineapple slices halfway through macerating time.

Preheat broiler (grill). Line a baking sheet with foil, arrange pineapple in single layer, and broil (grill) until lightly browned, about 5 minutes per side. Serve hot, topped with cooking juices and star anise, and garnished with lime wedges for squeezing.

To prepare: 20 minutes

To cook: 10 minutes, plus 30 minutes to macerate

4 servings

roasted apricot & vanilla tart

½ recipe Cornmeal Pastry (below)

1 egg white, lightly beaten

⅓ cup (3 oz/90 g) apricot jam

1 tsp cornstarch (cornflour)

8–10 firm, ripe apricots, pitted and cut into eighths

1 tsp vanilla extract (essence)

1 Tbsp superfine (caster) sugar

1 Tbsp powdered (icing) sugar

Preheat oven to 350°F (180°C). Roll out dough disk between 2 sheets of plastic wrap to form a round 12 inches (30 cm) in diameter. Remove plastic from top and carefully invert dough into a 10-inch (25-cm) tart pan. Press dough firmly and evenly into pan, ensuring that sides are not too thick. Run rolling pin over top to trim. Chill for 30 minutes in refrigerator or 10 minutes in freezer. Cover dough with a round of parchment (baking) paper or foil and fill with pie weights or dried beans. Bake until pastry is set, 20 minutes. Remove paper and weights and bake until lightly colored, 10 minutes more (line edges with foil if they are browning too fast). Brush with egg white and bake for 5 minutes more. Let cool on a wire rack.

Stir apricot jam and cornstarch together in a small bowl. Spread in pastry shell and arrange apricots on top. Stir vanilla and superfine sugar together and sprinkle over apricots. Bake until fruit is tender and bubbling, about 35 minutes. Serve warm or chilled, dusted with powdered sugar.

To prepare: 20 minutes, plus 40 minutes for pastry

To cook: 70 minutes

8 servings

cornmeal pastry

¾ cup (6 oz/185 g) cold butter, finely diced

3 cups (15 oz/470 g) all-purpose (plain) flour

½ cup (3½ oz/105 g) coarse cornmeal

3 Tbsp sugar

Pinch of salt

⅔ cup (5½ oz/170 g) plain low-fat or whole yogurt

Combine butter, flour, cornmeal, sugar, and salt in a food processor and pulse until mixture resembles fine crumbs. Or, in a bowl, work butter into dry ingredients with a pastry blender or 2 dinner knives. Add yogurt and continue to pulse or stir until mixture starts to come together in a ball. Do not overwork. Turn dough out onto a work surface covered with plastic wrap and press into 2 disks. Chill for at least 20 minutes, or freeze for about 10 minutes.

Note: Dough will keep in refrigerator for up to 5 days or in freezer for up to 3 months.

To prepare: 20 minutes, plus 20 minutes to chill

Enough dough for two 10-inch (25-cm) tarts or twelve 5½-inch (14-cm) tartlets

mango-passion sauce

Put the peeled flesh of 2 ripe mangoes in a blender. Add a little grated peeled fresh ginger, a splash of maple syrup, and a cupful of cold pineapple juice. Purée until smooth. Add a little passion fruit pulp, if available. Serve over sliced pineapple or persimmons.

peach melba

Gently poach peach halves in sugar syrup (made of equal parts water and sugar) until tender. Let cool. Purée fresh or thawed frozen raspberries with a little powdered (icing) sugar, then strain. Top peaches with a drizzle of raspberry sauce and serve, with vanilla sorbet if desired.

brandied kumquats

Use as a topping for ice cream or yogurt or a mix-in for fruit salads. Place washed kumquats in a clean jar with two-thirds of their volume of sugar. Add brandy to cover, seal tightly, and store in a cool, dark place for 1 month, turning jar occasionally.

caramel oranges

Gently melt sugar with a splash of water and 1 tsp lemon juice in a saucepan over medium-high heat. Cook without stirring until deep gold. Pour at once over peeled and sliced oranges. If eaten at once, the caramel will break into crunchy shards. The caramel will dissolve on standing.

carrot cupcakes with mascarpone icing

⅓ cup (3 oz/90 g) butter at room temperature

¾ cup (6 oz/185 g) granulated sugar

1 Tbsp maple syrup or honey

1 Tbsp finely grated orange zest

2 eggs

1 cup (4 oz/125 g) grated carrot

1 cup (5 oz/155 g) plus 2 Tbsp all-purpose (plain) flour

2 tsp baking powder

7 Tbsp (3½ fl oz/105 ml) fresh orange juice, warmed

1 tsp baking soda (bicarbonate of soda)

Mascarpone Icing

6 Tbsp (3 oz/90 g) butter at room temperature

1½ cups (6 oz/185 g) powdered (icing) sugar

1 tsp grated lemon zest

4 oz (125 g) cold mascarpone or low-fat cream cheese

Strips of dried mango for garnish (optional)

Preheat oven to 350°F (180°C). Line 10 standard muffin cups with paper liners.

Beat butter, granulated sugar, maple syrup, and orange zest together in a bowl until pale and creamy. Beat in eggs one at a time. Stir in carrot. Sift flour and baking powder together into a bowl. Stir orange juice and baking soda together in another small bowl. Stir flour mixture into creamed mixture in 2 additions alternately with orange juice mixture in 2 additions until smooth. Do not overbeat, or cupcakes will be tough.

Spoon batter into prepared muffin cups. Bake until cupcakes are risen and lightly golden, about 20 minutes. Let cupcakes stand for 10 minutes in pan on a wire rack, then turn out onto a baking sheet and let cool completely, about 1 hour.

For Icing: Cream butter and powdered sugar together in a bowl until light and fluffy. Stir in lemon zest and mascarpone until blended.

Once cupcakes are cooled, ice them and garnish with strips of dried mango, if desired.

Note: Store cupcakes in an airtight container for up to 3 days.

To prepare: 10 minutes

To cook: 20–25 minutes

10 cupcakes

golden kiwifruit pavlovas

Meringue(s)

4 egg whites (see Note) at room temperature

Pinch of salt

1 cup (7 oz/220 g) superfine (caster) sugar

1 tsp cornstarch (cornflour)

½ tsp malt vinegar

1 qt (32 fl oz/1 l) bottled passion fruit juice (see Notes)

1 cup (8 fl oz/250 ml) cold heavy (double) cream

1–2 Tbsp powdered (icing) sugar

4 or 5 golden kiwifruits, peeled and diced

Fresh passion fruit pulp for drizzling (optional)

Choose a baking day that is not humid to make pavlovas. Preheat oven to 325°F (165°C). Line a baking sheet with parchment (baking) paper.

For Meringue(s): In a large bowl, beat egg whites with salt until soft peaks form when the whisk is lifted. Gradually beat in superfine sugar and continue to beat until mixture is glossy and very thick and stiff peaks form when whisk is lifted. Beat in cornstarch and vinegar.

For individual meringues, use a large spoon to make 6–8 mounds of egg mixture on prepared pan, allowing 1–2 inches (2.5–5 cm) between them. For 1 large meringue, spoon into a single large mound. Swirl top(s) with a fork or icing spatula.

Bake for 2 minutes, then reduce oven temperature to 250°F (120°C). Continue to bake until crisp to the touch, about 1 hour for individual meringues and 1 hour and 40–50 minutes for a large meringue. Turn off oven and leave meringue(s) in oven to cool completely, about 2 hours or up to overnight. Store in an airtight container for up to 1 week.

Boil passion fruit juice in a saucepan over medium-high heat until reduced to ⅔ cup (5 fl oz/160 ml). Cover and chill thoroughly, at least 2 hours. It must be very cold before adding to cream. In a bowl, whip cream until soft peaks form. Fold in reduced juice and powdered sugar. Cover and chill until ready to serve.

To serve, top meringue(s) with flavored cream and sprinkle with diced kiwifruits. Drizzle with passion fruit pulp, if using.

Notes: For best results with any kind of meringue, the egg whites should not be too fresh—fresh whites make the mixture "bleed" a clear liquid. If you have access to fresh passion fruit, use it instead of the reduced juice. Simply halve fruit and scoop out seeds, pulp, and juice and fold into whipped cream. Sweeten to taste. If preferred, pulp can be strained to remove seeds.

To prepare: 35 minutes

To cook: 1 hour for individual desserts, 1 hour 40 minutes for a large pavlova; plus 3 hours to cool

6–8 individual pavlovas or 1 large pavlova

lemon soufflés

½ cup (4 oz/125 g) granulated sugar

½ cup (4 fl oz/125 ml) lemon juice

Finely grated zest of 1 lemon

½ tsp vanilla extract (essence)

2 egg whites at room temperature

¼ cup (2 oz/60 g) superfine
(caster) sugar

Powdered (icing) sugar for dusting

Preheat oven to 375°F (190°C). Combine granulated sugar, lemon juice, and zest in a saucepan and cook over medium heat, stirring occasionally, until sugar is dissolved. Reduce heat to low and simmer for 3 minutes. Remove from heat and stir in vanilla.

In a large bowl, beat egg whites until soft peaks form when the whisk is lifted. Gradually beat in superfine sugar and continue to beat until mixture is thick and glossy. Meanwhile, bring lemon mixture back to a boil. While whisking, add ¼ cup (2 fl oz/60 ml) hot lemon mixture into egg whites and beat until very light and fluffy, about 5 minutes.

Divide remaining lemon mixture among six 8–fl oz (250-ml) ramekins (about 2 teaspoons per cup). Divide egg whites among ramekins, making peaks on top with the back of a spoon. Bake until just beginning to brown, 5–6 minutes. Do not overcook, or soufflés will shrink as they cool. Remove from oven, dust with powdered sugar, and serve at once.

To prepare: 25 minutes

To cook: 5–6 minutes

6 individual soufflés

sweet potato pie

2 cups (6 oz/185 g) finely ground
graham crackers or other plain
cookie crumbs

2 tsp ground ginger

½ cup (4 oz/125 g) butter, melted

Filling

1 cup (8 oz/250 g) mashed or puréed
cooked sweet potato

1 cup (8 oz/250 g) low-fat sour cream

½ cup (3½ oz/105 g) packed
brown sugar

3 eggs

1 Tbsp dark molasses

1 Tbsp grated fresh ginger

1 tsp ground cinnamon

1 tsp ground allspice

Preheat oven to 325°F (165°C). Stir crumbs, ginger, and butter together in a bowl until blended. Press into bottom and sides of a 10-inch (25-cm) tart pan with removable bottom and chill for 30 minutes.

For Filling: Stir all filling ingredients together in a bowl until evenly blended. Remove chilled crust from refrigerator and press firmly into pan to compact it evenly. Spoon filling into crust. Bake until filling is set and springy to the touch and a skewer inserted in center comes out clean, about 45 minutes. Transfer pan to a wire rack and let cool. Unmold and chill for at least 1 hour.

Note: Pie will keep for up to 5 days in refrigerator.

To prepare: 30 minutes,
plus 30 minutes to chill

To cook: 45 minutes,
plus 1 hour to chill

8–10 servings

golden fruit bowl
with allspice syrup

Allspice Syrup

½ cup (4 oz/125 g) sugar

12 allspice berries

Zest of ½ orange, removed with a vegetable peeler

½ pineapple

2 oranges, peeled and segmented

½ cantaloupe, halved, seeded, and flesh cut into bite-sized chunks

For syrup: Combine sugar and ¾ cup (6 fl oz/180 ml) water in a small, heavy saucepan. Cook over medium heat, stirring until sugar is dissolved. Add allspice and orange zest and simmer gently for 10 minutes. Let cool, then strain through a fine-mesh sieve.

Cut peel from pineapple and trim away eyes. Remove core. Cut crosswise into slices, then cut into bite-sized chunks.

Put pineapple, oranges, and cantaloupe in a serving bowl. Pour syrup over fruit and refrigerate for at least 20 minutes or up to 4 hours.

To prepare: 20 minutes, plus 20 minutes to chill

To cook: 10 minutes

8 servings

golden cherry clafoutis

Batter

1 cup (8 fl oz/250 ml) low-fat or whole milk

3 eggs

⅔ cup (3½ oz/105 g) all-purpose (plain) flour

2 Tbsp granulated sugar

Pinch of salt

2 Tbsp Grand Marnier or other orange liqueur, or orange juice

Grated zest of ½ orange

1 tsp butter

2 tart apples, cored and thinly sliced

2 Tbsp granulated sugar

1 cup (4 oz/125 g) golden cherries, pitted if desired

1 Tbsp powdered (icing) sugar

Preheat oven to 425°F (220°C). Generously butter a 12-inch (30-cm) shallow baking dish.

For batter: Whisk milk, eggs, flour, granulated sugar, and salt together in a bowl until smooth. Stir in liqueur and zest. Strain through a fine-mesh sieve. Batter will be thin.

Melt butter in a frying pan over high heat. Add apple slices and sprinkle with granulated sugar. Sauté until softened, 3–4 minutes. Distribute apple slices evenly in prepared dish. Pour batter over apples and scatter with cherries (they will sink into batter). Bake until brown and lightly puffed, 30–35 minutes. Dust with powdered sugar and serve at once.

Variation: Use 1 cup (4 oz/125 g) fresh berries, such as blueberries, raspberries, or blackberries, in place of cherries.

To prepare: 35 minutes

To cook: 30–35 minutes

6 servings

cherries strawberries red plums

RED FRUITS AND VEGETABLES PROVIDE ANTIOXIDANTS

pomegranates ruby grapefruits

FOR PROTECTION AND HEALING • PROMOTE HEART

rhubarb cranberries red grapes

HEALTH • PROMOTE URINARY TRACT HEALTH • HELP

watermelons red apples quinces

REDUCE THE RISK OF CERTAIN CANCERS • IMPROVE

raspberries pink grapefruits red

MEMORY FUNCTION • RED FRUITS AND VEGETABLES

pears pomegranates red plums

OFFER ANTIOXIDANTS FOR PROTECTION AND HEALING

Red

Red is the color of ripeness, the deepest hue that many fruits reach after passing through stages of green or yellow. To take advantage of these fruits' colorful phytonutrients—some of which they share with blue fruits, at the other end of the color spectrum—leave them unpeeled whenever possible. You'll also reap the benefits of the extra fiber that the skin contains.

Red fruits are usually hard to find in the chilly weeks of early spring, since they need long, hot, sunny days to develop their full color. Strawberries, however, are at their jewel-like best at this time of year. Enjoy ripe strawberries adorned with only a sprinkle of sugar or a splash of cream, or with a drizzle of sweet balsamic vinegar for a greater flavor contrast (page 101). Or combine them with smooth, mild, naturally low-fat ricotta cheese in an updated English trifle (page 95).

Summertime brings the arrival of other red berries and cherries, fruits best enjoyed in their brief natural season. Cherries are delicious simmered into a rich-tasting filling for lacy crepes (page 102).

Other red fruits come into their own in autumn and winter. Less common fruits make an appearance at this time of year: pomegranates, with their hundreds of translucent ruby seeds, and quinces, which appear yellow-orange when raw but actually develop red-hued phytochemicals as they cook, turning color from a pink to ruby red.

SPRING	SUMMER	AUTUMN	WINTER
pink or ruby grapefruit	cherries	red apples	red apples
blood oranges	red grapes	cranberries	cranberries
red pears	red plums	red grapes	pink or ruby grapefruit
rhubarb	raspberries	red pears	red grapes
strawberries	rhubarb	red plums	blood oranges
	strawberries	pomegranates	red pears
	watermelon	quinces	pomegranates
		raspberries	quinces
		rhubarb	
		watermelon	

berry & ricotta trifles

1 cup (10 oz/315 g) raspberry or black currant jam

¼ cup (2 fl oz/60 ml) kirsch or sherry

¼ cup (2 fl oz/60 ml) orange juice

1½ cups (12 oz/375 g) ricotta cheese

¼ cup (1 oz/30 g) powdered (icing) sugar

1 tsp vanilla extract (essence)

1 sponge cake, purchased or homemade (below), 7 inches (18 cm) in diameter, cut into 1-inch (2.5-cm) cubes

4 cups (1 lb/500 g) strawberries, cored and sliced

If desired, push raspberry jam through a sieve with back of a large spoon to remove seeds. Stir jam, kirsch, and orange juice together in a small bowl. Purée ricotta, sugar, and vanilla in a blender until smooth.

Divide half of cake cubes among 6 serving glasses. Drizzle one-third of jam mixture evenly over sponge cake. Top with one-third of strawberries, then half of ricotta mixture. Repeat with layers of sponge cake, jam mixture, berries, and ricotta. Top with a final layer of strawberries and spoon the remaining third of jam mixture over all.

Cover and chill for at least 1 hour before serving.

Note: Trifles can be covered and stored for up to 12 hours in refrigerator.

To prepare: 20 minutes, plus 1 hour to chill

6 servings

sponge cake

3 eggs at room temperature

¾ cup (5 oz/155 g) superfine (caster) sugar

Pinch of salt

¾ cup (3 oz/90 g) cake (soft-wheat) flour

¼ cup (1 oz/30 g) cornstarch (cornflour)

1 tsp baking powder

3 Tbsp butter, melted and cooled

Preheat oven to 350°F (180°C). Line a 7-inch (18-cm) cake pan with parchment (baking) paper to cover bottom and sides.

With an electric mixer on high speed, beat eggs, sugar, and salt together until they reach a thick, creamy ribbonlike texture, 15 minutes. Sift flour, cornstarch, and baking powder together. Using a large slotted spoon, gently fold dry ingredients into egg mixture, one-third at a time. Gently fold in butter.

Pour batter into prepared pan and bake until cake springs back when lightly pressed, 30–35 minutes. Remove from oven and let cool in pan on a wire rack. Turn out and wrap in plastic wrap when completely cool.

Note: Sponge cake will keep in the refrigerator for 5 days or can be frozen for up to 2 months.

To prepare: 30 minutes

To cook: 30 minutes, plus 40 minutes to cool

One 7-inch (18-cm) cake, 6–8 servings

plum cake

Vegetable oil spray

1½ cups (7½ oz/235 g) all-purpose (plain) flour

1 teaspoon baking powder

¼ teaspoon salt

1 cup (8 oz/250 g) butter at room temperature

1 cup (8 oz/250 g) plus 1 Tbsp sugar

2 large eggs at room temperature

6–8 plums (about 1 lb/500 g), halved, pitted, and each half cut into 4 slices

¼ teaspoon ground cinnamon

Place a rack in lower third of oven and preheat to 350°F (180°C). Coat a 9-inch (23-cm) round or 8-inch (20-cm) square cake pan with vegetable oil spray. Line bottom with parchment (baking) paper and coat paper with more spray.

Whisk together flour, baking powder, and salt. With an electric mixer, beat together butter and 1 cup sugar until pale and fluffy. Add eggs one at a time, beating well after each addition. Add flour mixture and mix well.

Pour batter into prepared pan and spread evenly. Poke plum slices into the batter, placing them close together. In a small bowl, combine cinnamon and 1 Tbsp sugar, and sprinkle over surface.

Bake until top is golden, edges pull away from pan, and a skewer inserted in center comes out clean, 50–60 minutes. Let cool for about 30 minutes before serving.

Note: Other stone fruits can be used in place of the plums, such as apricots, nectarines, and peaches. Store cake in an airtight container in the refrigerator for up to 3 days or freeze for up to 2 months.

To prepare: 30 minutes

To cook: 50 minutes, plus 30 minutes to cool

8 servings

raspberry jellies

1 Tbsp (1 envelope) unflavored powdered gelatin

3 cups (24 fl oz/750 ml) cranberry cocktail or grape juice, chilled

2 cups (12 oz/375 g) raspberries or seedless red grapes

In a cup or small bowl, sprinkle gelatin over ¼ cup (2 fl oz/60 ml) water and let stand until absorbed, about 3 minutes. Heat in microwave for about 20 seconds or in a small saucepan over low heat on stove top for about 1 minute to dissolve. Stir well to ensure that gelatin is fully dissolved. In a bowl, combine gelatin and 1 cup (8 fl oz/250 ml) juice and mix well. Chill for 20 minutes. Add remaining 2 cups (16 fl oz/500 ml) juice, stirring to blend well. Divide raspberries among six 8–fl oz (250-ml) serving glasses or bowls. Pour juice mixture over fruit. Cover with plastic wrap and chill until fully set, about 4 hours or up to 2 days.

Note: Sparkling grape or apple juice and green grapes can also be used for these jellies.

To prepare: 30 minutes, plus 4 hours to set

6 servings

cherries flambéed in rum

½ cup (5 oz/155 g) red currant or
raspberry jam

3 Tbsp sugar

1 Tbsp lemon juice

1 lb (500 g) fresh cherries, stemmed
and pitted if desired (see Note)

⅓ cup (3 fl oz/80 ml) rum or kirsch

Crème fraîche for serving

Push and smear jam through a fine-mesh sieve with back of a large spoon to remove seeds. Combine jam, sugar, ½ cup (4 fl oz/125 ml) water, and lemon juice in a large, heavy nonreactive saucepan. Simmer over medium heat until slightly syrupy, 2–3 minutes. Add cherries and simmer until slightly softened, 2–3 minutes more. Add a little water if mixture starts to caramelize. Divide hot fruit among serving glasses and spoon syrup over it. Heat rum in a microwave for 20 seconds or in a small saucepan over low heat for 1–2 minutes. Away from open flame, pour rum over fruit and carefully ignite fumes with a long match. Serve with crème fraîche.

Note: The cherries look prettier with their stems attached but will be easier to eat if they are pitted. This recipe is also a great way to prepare peeled, fresh peach halves, in which case use apricot jam.

To prepare: 15 minutes

To cook: 10 minutes

4 servings

rhubarb fool

2½ cups (10 oz/315 g) ½-inch
(12-mm) lengths rhubarb
(8 or 9 stalks)

¾ cup (6 oz/185 g) granulated sugar,
plus more if needed

1½ cups (12 fl oz/375 ml) heavy
(double) cream

1½ Tbsp powdered (icing) sugar

1 Tbsp kirsch or raspberry brandy
(optional)

In a saucepan, combine rhubarb, ⅔ cup (5 fl oz/160 ml) water, and granulated sugar. Cover and cook over low heat, stirring occasionally, until rhubarb is tender and breaks up easily, about 8 minutes. Purée in a food processor or blender. Taste and add more sugar if needed. Cover and chill for least 1 hour or for up to 3 days.

In a deep bowl, whip cream with powdered sugar until soft peaks form when the whisk is lifted. Stir in kirsch, if using. Spoon cream and rhubarb purée into martini glasses or tall serving glasses in alternate layers, swirling a fork gently through layers to combine them slightly. Chill for at least 30 minutes before serving.

Note: Other acidic fruit purées, such as plum, gooseberry, and raspberry, can be used in place of rhubarb.

*To prepare: 20 minutes,
plus 1½ hours to chill*

To cook: 8 minutes

5 or 6 servings

cookie & berry "tartlets"

Cookies make a great dessert base for fresh berries. Spread shortbread or other thin, crisp cookies with a little jam and arrange fresh raspberries in a circular pattern on top. Serve with raspberry purée if desired.

slow-baked quinces

Put whole or halved peeled quinces in a baking dish and add a generous splash of red wine and a liberal sprinkling of sugar. Cover and bake in a 325°F (165°C) oven for about 4 hours, topping up the liquid from time to time as needed.

strawberries with balsamic

Balsamic vinegar is a delicious and surprising complement to strawberries. Choose an aged true balsamic and the smallest, ripest red berries you can find. Drizzle the strawberries with balsamic and sprinkle with black pepper.

mixed berry compote

Simmer fresh or frozen raspberries or a mixture of berries with a couple of bay leaves, a cinnamon stick, a vanilla bean, and sugar to taste. Cook gently until slightly syrupy, about 30 minutes. Add a little lemon juice.

brandied berry crepes

Crepe Batter

⅔ cup (3½ oz/105 g) all-purpose (plain) flour

1 Tbsp sugar

¼ tsp salt

1 cup (8 fl oz/250 ml) cold low-fat or whole milk

1 egg

1 egg yolk

2 Tbsp butter, melted

1 tsp vanilla extract (essence)

2 Tbsp butter, or as needed

Filling

2 cups (8 oz/250 g) raspberries

¼ cup (2 oz/60 g) sugar

1 Tbsp cornstarch (cornflour) mixed with ¼ cup (2 fl oz/60 ml) brandy

1 Tbsp lemon juice

2 cups (8 oz/250 g) mixed fresh red berries, such as pitted cherries, stemmed red currants, cranberries, and cored and sliced strawberries

For Batter: Whisk all batter ingredients together in a bowl until smooth. Strain through a fine-mesh sieve to remove any lumps. Let stand for at least 15 minutes, or cover and refrigerate for up to 8 hours.

Melt a little of the 2 Tbsp butter in a crepe pan or small frying pan over medium-high heat and cook until butter smells nutty and just starts to brown. Pour in a small ladleful (3 Tbsp) of batter and quickly tilt pan to coat bottom evenly. Cook just until batter is set and golden on bottom, then flip and cook on second side for another minute or two. Repeat to make 8 crepes, brushing pan with more butter as needed. Stack cooked crepes on a plate. If not using at once, let cool, cover with plastic wrap, and let stand for up to 2 hours or refrigerate for up to 12 hours.

For Filling: Combine raspberries and sugar in a saucepan and cook over medium heat, stirring, until sugar is dissolved. Reduce heat to maintain a simmer, stir in brandy mixture, and cook, stirring, until slightly thickened. Stir in lemon juice. Strain through a fine-mesh sieve. If not serving crepes at once, let sauce cool, cover, and refrigerate for up to 5 days.

To serve, bring sauce to a simmer and add 2 cups mixed fruits. Return to a simmer, then remove from heat. Reheat crepes in microwave for 30 seconds or in low (200°F/95°C) oven covered with foil for 10 minutes. (If crepes have been chilled, reheat for 1 minute in microwave or 15 minutes in 350°F/180°C oven.)

Spoon filling into each crepe and fold into quarters. Serve at once.

To prepare: 30 minutes

To cook: 15 minutes

8 filled crepes, 4 servings

pear & frangipane galettes

½ recipe Pastry Shell (page 34)

2 Tbsp butter

3 red-skinned pears, cored and diced

1 Tbsp sugar

Frangipane Filling

1¼ cups (5 oz/155 g) ground almonds

⅓ cup (3 oz/90 g) butter, softened

⅓ cup (3 oz/90 g) sugar

1 tsp kirsch (optional)

¼ tsp almond extract (essence)

1 egg

Thyme sprigs for garnish (optional)

Roll out pastry on a lightly floured work surface to ⅛ inch (3 mm) thick. Cut out six 5-inch (13-cm) rounds, rerolling pastry as needed. Place rounds on a baking sheet lined with parchment (baking) paper, allowing a little space between them, and chill until ready to bake.

Preheat oven to 350°F (180°C). Melt butter in a heavy frying pan over medium-high heat and cook until it bubbles and starts to brown. Add pears and sugar and cook, tossing frequently, until lightly browned, about 1–2 minutes. Let cool.

For Filling: Whisk all filling ingredients together in a bowl until evenly combined. Spread 2 Tbsp filling on each pastry round, leaving a ½-inch (12-mm) margin around edge. Top each with the cooled pears, dividing evenly. Crimp pastry edges. Bake until golden and cooked through, about 30 minutes. Garnish with thyme sprigs, if desired, and serve.

To prepare: 10 minutes

To cook: 30 minutes

6 servings

raspberries in red wine syrup

1 cup (8 fl oz/250 ml) dry red wine such as Merlot

½ cup (4 fl oz/125 ml) port

¾ cup (6 oz/185 g) sugar

6 whole cloves

1 cinnamon stick

6 cardamom pods

3 cups (12 oz/375 g) raspberries

2 tsp best-quality unsweetened cocoa powder (optional)

Combine all ingredients except the raspberries and cocoa in a saucepan. Bring to a simmer over medium heat, stirring until sugar is dissolved. Reduce heat to low and simmer until syrupy and reduced by half, 20–25 minutes. Let cool slightly or completely.

Spoon syrup onto serving plates and top with a mound of raspberries. Dust with cocoa powder, if desired.

Note: The syrup can be made in quantity and refrigerated in a covered container for up to 4 weeks. It is also excellent with fresh figs.

To prepare: 5 minutes

To cook: 20–25 minutes

4 servings

ruby grapefruit sorbet

2 tsp unflavored powdered gelatin

1 cup (8 oz/250 g) sugar

¼ cup (2 fl oz/60 ml) lemon juice, strained

2½ cups (20 fl oz/625 ml) ruby grapefruit juice

¼ cup (2 fl oz/60 ml) orange juice

2 egg whites

In a cup, sprinkle gelatin over ¼ cup (2 fl oz/60 ml) cold water and let stand until absorbed, about 3 minutes. Combine sugar and ½ cup (4 fl oz/125 ml) cold water in a saucepan and simmer for 5 minutes, stirring, until sugar is dissolved. Remove from heat and stir in gelatin mixture until dissolved. Let cool, then stir in fruit juices. Pour into a shallow metal baking pan and freeze until mixture begins to solidify, about 2 hours. Transfer to a food processor or bowl and pulse or beat with an electric mixer or whisk to break up. Add egg whites and continue beating until light and fluffy. Cover and freeze until firm, at least 4 hours. If frozen for more than 48 hours before using, beat again, then refreeze for 4 hours for best consistency.

To prepare: 30 minutes, plus 6 hours to freeze

To cook: 5 minutes

About 1 quart, 6–8 servings

red currant filo tarts

6 sheets thawed frozen filo pastry, about 20 x 12 inches (50 x 30 cm) each

¼ cup (2 oz/60 g) butter, melted

¼ cup (2 oz/60 g) granulated sugar

2 Tbsp red currant or raspberry jelly

2 cups (8 oz/250 g) stemmed fresh red currants, raspberries, or cored and sliced strawberries

1 Tbsp powdered (icing) sugar

Preheat oven to 325°F (165°C). Lay a sheet of filo on a baking sheet; keep remaining filo covered with a towel. Brush filo sheet with a little butter and sprinkle with a little granulated sugar. Top with another sheet, brush with butter, and sprinkle with sugar. Repeat with remaining filo, stacking layers and ending with a brushing of butter only. Press filo stack firmly and evenly to compact layers. Using a sharp knife, cut out six 5-inch (13-cm) rounds. Butter six 4-inch (10-cm) tart pans and press a filo round into each. Sprinkle with remaining granulated sugar.

Bake until crisp and golden, about 20 minutes. Transfer pans to wire racks and let cool to the touch. Remove filo shells from pans and let cool completely on wire racks. Use at once, or store in an airtight container at room temperature for up to 5 days. Crisp in a warm oven for 5–10 minutes, if necessary.

Up to an hour before serving, whisk jelly in a bowl to soften. Add berries and stir gently to combine. Spoon into filo shells. Dust with powdered sugar just before serving.

To prepare: 15 minutes

To cook: 20 minutes

6 servings

cashews pistachio nuts polenta

WHOLE GRAINS, LEGUMES, SEEDS, AND NUTS PROMOTE

coffee macadamia nuts pecans

ARTERY AND HEART HEALTH • HELP REDUCE THE RISK

almonds peanuts whole wheat

OF DIABETES • REDUCE HIGH BLOOD PRESSURE • OFFER

oats chestnuts dark chocolate

ANTIOXIDANTS FOR PROTECTION AND HEALING • HELP

hazelnuts pine nuts brown rice

REDUCE THE RISK OF STROKE • MAY REDUCE THE RISK

walnuts cashews pistachio nuts

OF CANCERS OF THE BREAST, PROSTATE, AND COLON

Brown

This down-to-earth chapter of the healthy-eating rainbow is devoted not to fruits or vegetables, but to a distinctive group of healthful foods that come from plants: grains and seeds. Nuts are a type of seed that lend themselves well to sweet preparations. Two particular seeds—the coffee bean and the cocoa bean—are unique in their antioxidant benefits and widespread appeal, bordering on obsession.

Grains might not leap to mind when you think about dessert, but they can play a number of roles. Old-fashioned rolled oats make a crunchy streusel topping for fruit crisps (page 123), and stone-ground corn-meal adds texture to a rustic polenta cake (page 124) and a golden, sweet pastry crust (page 79).

Coffee is currently being studied for its beneficial effects against a range of ailments. Some benefits derive from caffeine, others from coffee's rich phytochemical content. Unless you are particularly sensitive to caffeine, you needn't feel that a coffee or chocolate dessert is a guilty pleasure. On a summer evening, an espresso granita (page 119) combines dessert and coffee into one simple and refreshing ending to a meal.

Nuts, a highly nutritious member of the brown group, are marvelous additions to a number of sweet dishes. Rice pudding with pistachios (page 120) and hazelnut-dotted Prune Panforte (page 113) are especially good made with new-harvest nuts in fall.

GRAINS	LEGUMES	NUTS	OTHER
oats	peanuts	almonds	coffee
polenta (corn)		Brazil nuts	dark chocolate
brown rice		cashews	
whole wheat		chestnuts	
		hazelnuts	
		macadamia nuts	
		pecans	
		pine nuts	
		pistachio nuts	
		walnuts	

prune panforte

1 cup (5½ oz/170 g) almonds

1 cup (5 oz/155 g) hazelnuts (filberts)

2 cups (12 oz/375 g) pitted prunes or mixed prunes and dried figs, diced

⅔ cup (4 oz/125 g) all-purpose (plain) flour

2 Tbsp unsweetened cocoa powder

2 tsp ground cinnamon

1 tsp ground allspice

¼ tsp freshly grated nutmeg

1 tsp ground ginger

½ cup (6 oz/185 g) honey

½ cup (4 oz/125 g) granulated sugar

2 oz (60 g) semisweet (plain) chocolate, chopped

Powdered (icing) sugar for dusting

Preheat oven to 300°F (150°C). Grease a 9-inch (23-cm) springform pan and line bottom with parchment (baking) paper. Spread almonds and hazelnuts on baking sheets and toast for 20 minutes, shaking the pans every 5 minutes. Pour hazelnuts into a clean kitchen towel and rub together to remove skins. Coarsely chop almonds and halve hazelnuts. Stir nuts, dried fruit, flour, cocoa powder, and spices together in a bowl.

Heat honey and granulated sugar in a saucepan over medium-high heat until sugar is dissolved, then boil to 234°F (112°C) on a candy thermometer or until a small amount of mixture dropped into very cold water forms a soft ball that flattens when removed from water. Remove from heat, add chocolate, and stir until smooth. Pour into nut mixture and quickly stir with a sturdy wooden spoon until combined. Work quickly, as mixture thickens fast. Press into prepared pan and bake until set, about 35 minutes. Let cool slightly in pan on a wire rack, but remove from pan while still warm and let cool completely on rack. Dust with powdered sugar and cut into thin slices to serve.

Note: Store in an airtight container for 3–4 weeks.

To prepare: 25 minutes

To cook: 35 minutes, plus 2 hours to cool

20 servings

brazil nut & almond torte

1 cup (3 oz/90 g) finely ground graham crackers or other plain cookie crumbs

1¼ cups (10 oz/315 g) sugar

2 tsp baking powder

1 cup (5 oz/155 g) Brazil nuts, finely chopped

1 cup (4 oz/125 g) sliced almonds, finely chopped

1 cup (6 oz/185 g) pitted dates, finely chopped

3 oz (90 g) bittersweet (plain) chocolate, finely chopped, or ½ cup (3 oz/90 g) chocolate chips

8 egg whites

Preheat oven to 325°F (165°C). Butter a 9-inch (23-cm) springform pan and line bottom with parchment (baking) paper. Sprinkle bottom with cookie crumbs. Stir sugar and baking powder together in a bowl. Add nuts and dates. Break up dates with your fingertips so they are evenly distributed. Stir in chocolate.

In a large bowl, beat egg whites until stiff, glossy peaks form when the whisk is lifted. Fold in nut mixture until evenly blended. Spoon into prepared pan and smooth top. Bake until firm to the touch, about 1½ hours. Let cool completely in pan on a wire rack for at least 2 hours.

Unlatch pan sides and transfer cake to a plate. Cut into wedges to serve.

Note: Store leftover cake wrapped tightly in foil in an airtight container at room temperature for several weeks.

To prepare: 45 minutes

To cook: 1½ hours, plus 2 hours to cool

16 servings

almond cake
with kirsch syrup

1¼ cups (10 oz/315 g) sugar

6 large eggs, separated

Finely grated zest of 1 lemon

Finely grated zest of ½ orange

1 cup (5 oz/155 g) ground almonds

½ cup (2½ oz/75 g) all-purpose (plain) flour

1 tsp baking powder

1 tsp almond extract (essence)

Kirsch Syrup

3 Tbsp kirsch

1 Tbsp lemon juice

2 Tbsp sugar

Preheat oven to 325°F (165°C). Butter a 9-inch (23-cm) springform pan and line bottom with parchment (baking) paper.

Beat sugar, egg yolks, and zests together in a large bowl with an electric mixer until thick and pale, about 10 minutes. Stir almonds, flour, and baking powder together in a small bowl. Add to egg yolk mixture with almond extract and stir to blend.

In a deep metal bowl, beat egg whites until soft peaks form when the whisk is lifted. Gently fold whites into egg yolk mixture. Pour into prepared pan and carefully smooth top without deflating batter. Bake until cake springs back when lightly touched, 60–65 minutes. Unlatch sides of pan and transfer cake onto a wire rack while hot.

For Kirsch Syrup: Combine kirsch, lemon juice, and sugar in a small nonreactive saucepan. Cook over medium heat, stirring until sugar is dissolved. Remove from heat and brush hot syrup gently and evenly over cake. Let cool completely before serving.

Notes: Serve with pitted fresh cherries or raspberries and crème fraîche, or split in half horizontally and fill with chopped pitted fresh cherries folded into a little whipped chilled cream. Store cake in a covered container at room temperature for up to 5 days.

To prepare: 20 minutes

To cook: 1 hour

10–12 servings

hazelnut macaroons

1 cup (5 oz/155 g) hazelnuts (filberts)

5 egg whites at room temperature

Pinch of salt

1 cup (7 oz/220 g) superfine (caster) sugar

1½ cups (6 oz/185 g) powdered (icing) sugar, sifted

1 tsp baking powder

1 tsp vanilla extract (essence)

Choose a baking day that is not humid to make macaroons. Preheat oven to 325°F (165°C). Spread hazelnuts in a single layer on a baking sheet. Toast for 20 minutes, shaking pan every 5 minutes. Pour nuts into a clean kitchen towel and rub together to remove skins. Let cool completely, then chop finely with a chef's knife (do not do this in a processor, or nuts will release too much oil and become pasty). Leave oven on.

In a large bowl, beat egg whites with salt until soft peaks form when the whisk is lifted. Gradually beat in superfine sugar until stiff, glossy peaks form. Stir powdered sugar and baking powder together in a bowl until blended. Fold into egg whites with vanilla, then fold in cooled nuts with a metal spoon. Do not beat, or oils in nuts will deflate the mixture.

Line baking sheets with parchment (baking) paper. Place teaspoonfuls of batter on prepared pans, allowing a little space between them. Place pans in oven and immediately lower oven temperature to 250°F (120°C). Bake until macaroons are dry and crisp, about 1 hour. Turn off oven and leave macaroons in oven to cool completely, about 2 hours or up to overnight.

Note: If you like, dip macaroons in melted chocolate and sprinkle with chopped hazelnuts, or serve with fresh raspberries and raspberry sauce (see page 80).

To prepare: 45 minutes

To cook: 1 hour, plus 2 hours to cool

About 60 macaroons

real hot chocolate

2 cups (16 fl oz/250 ml) low-fat or whole milk

2½ oz (75 g) best-quality bittersweet chocolate, finely chopped

1½ Tbsp sugar

1 cinnamon stick

1–2 Tbsp Kahlúa or other coffee liqueur (optional)

In a saucepan, combine milk, chocolate, sugar, and cinnamon. Cook over low heat, stirring to dissolve sugar, until bubbles form around edges of pan. Discard cinnamon and whisk mixture until frothy. Whisk in Kahlúa, if using. Pour into cups and serve at once.

To prepare: 10 minutes

To cook: 5 minutes

2 servings

chocolate-dipped strawberries

Chop dark chocolate into small pieces and melt in a saucepan over low heat. Dip strawberries in melted chocolate to coat three-fourths of each fruit. Place on parchment (baking) paper to set. Serve on same day.

affogato

For this Italian favorite combining ice cream and hot coffee, put a scoop of vanilla ice cream in a heatproof tumbler and garnish with broken praline, if you like. Serve a shot of espresso alongside for diners to pour over the ice cream.

caramelized hazelnuts & harvest fruits

Sauté sliced pears and apples in a little butter and brown sugar until they start to caramelize. Mix in generous handfuls toasted hazelnuts (filberts) and almonds and chopped dates. Serve with a dollop of crème fraîche, if desired.

espresso granita

Pour 2 cups (16 fl oz/500 ml) strong, sweetened coffee into a shallow metal pan and freeze until slushy, stirring occasionally. Draw a fork through mixture when it is frozen to break it up into icy crystals. Scoop into serving glasses.

chocolate-pumpkin cake

1 cup (8 oz/250 g) granulated sugar

1 egg

½ cup (4 fl oz/125 ml) low-fat or whole milk or plain yogurt

1 cup (4 oz/125 g) packed shredded raw pumpkin (see Note)

⅓ cup (1 oz/30 g) best-quality unsweetened cocoa powder

½ cup (3 oz/90 g) chocolate chips

½ cup (4 oz/125 g) butter, softened

1 tsp baking soda (bicarbonate of soda)

1 tsp vanilla extract (essence)

2 cups (8 oz/250 g) cake (soft-wheat) flour

2 tsp baking powder

½ cup (4 fl oz/125 ml) strong, hot coffee

Powdered (icing) sugar for dusting

Preheat oven to 325°F (165°C). Butter a 9-inch (23-cm) round cake pan and line bottom with parchment (baking) paper.

Combine all ingredients except powdered sugar in a food processor and process to blend, 30–40 seconds, or beat in a bowl with an electric mixer or by hand. Pour into prepared pan and smooth top.

Bake until cake is risen and set and a skewer inserted in center comes out clean, about 50 minutes. Let cool in pan on a wire rack. Remove from pan and dust with powdered sugar. Cut into wedges to serve.

Note: The magic ingredient in this cake is grated raw pumpkin. Its color and flavor are indiscernible in the baked cake but it creates a moist texture. If preferred, the same amount of shredded carrot can be used instead of pumpkin. Store cake in a sealed container at room temperature for up to a week.

To prepare: 15 minutes

To cook: 50 minutes

8–10 servings

pistachio rice pudding

5 cups (40 fl oz/1.25 l) low-fat or whole milk

½ cup (4 fl oz/125 ml) sweetened condensed milk

1 cup (7 oz/220 g) short-grain rice, preferably organic

½ tsp ground cardamom

1 tsp vanilla extract (essence)

½ cup (3 oz/90 g) dried apricots, chopped

Grated zest of ½ lemon

2 Tbsp heavy (double) cream (optional)

½ cup (2 oz/60 g) pistachios, chopped

Combine milk, condensed milk, and rice in a saucepan and bring to a boil over medium heat. Reduce heat to maintain a low simmer and cook, stirring occasionally, for 10 minutes. Add cardamom, vanilla, and two-thirds of apricots and cook until rice is tender, stirring occasionally, about 10 minutes. Stir in lemon zest and cream, if using.

Serve warm or cold, garnished with pistachios and remaining apricots. To serve cold, press parchment (baking) paper directly onto surface to prevent a skin from forming and chill for at least 3–4 hours or up to 24 hours. The pudding will thicken on cooling.

To prepare: 15 minutes

To cook: 20 minutes

6 servings

oatmeal pear crisp

5 firm, just-ripe pears

1 Tbsp granulated sugar

2 tsp cornstarch (cornflour)

2 Tbsp lemon juice

½ cup (3½ oz/105 g) packed brown sugar

1 cup (3 oz/90 g) old-fashioned rolled oats

¼ cup (1 oz/30 g) oat bran

⅔ cup (3½ oz/105 g) all-purpose (plain) flour

1 tsp baking powder

½ tsp cardamom seeds, finely ground

7 Tbsp (3½ oz/105 g) butter

Yogurt or crème fraîche for serving

Preheat oven to 350°F (180°C). Quarter, core, and thinly slice pears. Sprinkle with granulated sugar and cornstarch and toss gently. Spread slices in an even layer in a shallow baking dish 12 inches (30 cm) in diameter. Sprinkle with lemon juice.

Stir brown sugar, oats, oat bran, flour, baking powder, and cardamom together in a bowl. Finely chop butter and rub into oat mixture with your fingertips until mixture is crumbly, or process mixture in a food processor until crumbly. Sprinkle evenly over fruit. Bake until golden and crisp, about 40 minutes. Serve hot or warm, scooped into bowls and topped with a dollop of yogurt or crème fraîche.

Note: If cardamom seeds are unavailable, but green pods are, you will need to open 2 pods to get ½ tsp seeds.

To prepare: 15 minutes

To cook: 40 minutes

6 servings

bread puddings

2 cups (16 fl oz/500 ml) low-fat or whole milk

3 eggs

¼ cup (2 oz/60 g) sugar

½ tsp freshly grated nutmeg

2 tsp vanilla extract (essence)

2 Tbsp butter, softened

7 slices bread, preferably light whole wheat (wholemeal)

1 large or 2 small tart apples, peeled, cored, and thinly sliced

⅓ cup (2 oz/60 g) raisins

¼ cup (1 oz/30 g) sliced almonds

Whisk milk, eggs, sugar, nutmeg, and vanilla together in a bowl until blended. Coat a shallow 12-inch (30-cm) baking dish with a little butter. Remove crusts from bread and spread bread lightly with remaining butter. Cut each slice into 4 triangles. Interleave bread triangles with apple slices in a single layer in prepared dish. Sprinkle with raisins and almonds. Pour egg mixture into dish. Let stand at room temperature for 15 minutes or refrigerate for up to 4 hours.

Preheat oven to 350°F (180°C). Bake pudding until puffed and golden, about 40 minutes. Serve hot or at room temperature.

Note: You can also bake mixture in four to six 12–fl oz (375-ml) ramekins for 25–30 minutes.

To prepare: 30 minutes, plus 15 minutes to stand

To cook: 40 minutes

5 or 6 servings

walnut & date tart

1 cup (6 oz/185 g) pitted dates, chopped

1 cup (8 fl oz/250 ml) orange juice

½ cup (5 oz/155 g) light corn syrup

2 eggs, lightly beaten

½ cup (4 oz/125 g) light sour cream

2 tsp cornstarch (cornflour)

1 partially baked 10-inch (25-cm) Pastry Shell (page 34)

1 cup (4 oz/125 g) walnut or pecan halves

Sliced pears and whipped cream for serving (optional)

Preheat oven to 350°F (180°C). Combine dates and orange juice in a saucepan and simmer over low heat until dates are soft and pulpy, about 5 minutes. Remove from heat and whisk in corn syrup and eggs. Stir sour cream and cornstarch together in a small bowl and whisk into date mixture. Pour into pastry shell and sprinkle with nuts. Bake until filling has set in center, about 1 hour.

Let cool in pan on a wire rack, then chill for at least 1 hour. Unmold and cut into slender wedges. Serve wedges with pears and whipped cream, if desired.

Note: This filling can also be used for tartlets. Use 8 partially baked 4½-inch (11.5-cm) pastry shells and bake for 35–40 minutes.

To prepare: 15 minutes, plus 1 hour for pastry shell

To cook: 1 hour, plus 1 hour to chill

10–12 servings

polenta cake

1½ cups (12 oz/375 g) granulated sugar

2 eggs

Grated zest and juice of 2 lemons

1 cup (8 fl oz/250 ml) canola oil

¾ cup (6 oz/185 g) low-fat yogurt

1½ cups (7½ oz/235 g) all-purpose (plain) flour

2 tsp baking powder

1 cup (7 oz/220 g) instant polenta

2 cups (8 oz/250 g) fresh or frozen blackberries, plus fresh blackberries for garnish (optional)

Powdered (icing) sugar for dusting

Crème fraîche for serving

Preheat oven to 325°F (165°C). Butter a 9-inch (23-cm) springform pan and line bottom with parchment (baking) paper.

Whisk together granulated sugar, eggs, lemon zest and juice, oil, and yogurt in a bowl. In another bowl, stir flour, baking powder, and polenta together. Gradually stir dry ingredients into wet ingredients until just combined. Fold in blackberries. Pour into prepared pan and smooth top. Bake until springy to touch, about 1½ hours.

Let cool in pan on a wire rack before unlatching sides of pan and transferring cake to a serving plate. Dust with powdered sugar and cut into wedges to serve, accompanied with crème fraîche and berries, if using.

Note: Store cake in a covered container in refrigerator for up to 5 days.

To prepare: 10 minutes

To cook: 1½ hours

16 servings

Nutrients at work

Humans need more than forty nutrients to support life. Many foods are good sources of many different nutrients, but no single food provides everything. Eating a variety of foods, preferably in their whole form, is the best way to get all the nutrients your body needs. Some nutrients require others for optimal absorption, but excessive amounts may result in heath problems.

Until recently, nutritionists recommended the distribution of carbohydrates, protein, and fat in a well-balanced diet to be 55 percent of calories from carbohydrates, 15 percent of calories from protein, and 30 percent of calories from fat. As we have learned more about individual health needs and differences in metabolism, we have become more flexible in determining what constitutes a healthy diet. The table below shows macronutrient ranges recommended by the Institute of Medicine, part of the U.S. National Academies. These ranges are more likely to accommodate everyone's health needs.

To help you evaluate and balance your diet as you prepare the recipes in this book, turn to pages 130–33 for nutritional analyses of each recipe.

Nutrition experts have also determined guidelines for vitamins and minerals. For more information, see pages 128–29.

CARBOHYDRATES, PROTEIN, AND FATS

NUTRIENTS AND FOOD SOURCES	FUNCTIONS	RECOMMENDED % OF DAILY CALORIES AND GUIDANCE
Carbohydrates COMPLEX CARBOHYDRATES • Grains, breads, cereals, pastas • Dried beans and peas, lentils • Starchy vegetables (potatoes, corn, green peas)	• Main source of energy for the body • Particularly important for the brain and nervous system • Fiber aids normal digestion	45–65% • Favor complex carbohydrates, especially legumes, vegetables, and whole grains (brown rice; whole-grain bread, pasta, and cereal). • Many foods high in complex carbohydrates are also good fiber sources. Among the best are bran cereals, canned and dried beans, dried fruit, and rolled oats. Recommended daily intake of fiber for adults under age 50 is 25 g for women and 38 g for men. For women over age 50, intake is 21 g; for men, 30 g.
SIMPLE CARBOHYDRATES • Naturally occurring sugars in fruits, vegetables, and milk • Added refined sugars in soft drinks, candy, baked goods, jams and jellies, etc.	• Provide energy	• Fruit and vegetables have naturally occurring sugars but also have vitamins, minerals, and phytochemicals. Refined sugar, on the other hand, has little to offer in the way of nutrition, so limit your intake to get the most from your daily calories.

Source: Institute of Medicine. Dietary Reference Intakes for Energy, Carbohydrates, Fiber, Fat, Protein and Amino Acids (Macronutrients).

NUTRIENTS AND FOOD SOURCES	FUNCTIONS	RECOMMENDED % OF DAILY CALORIES AND GUIDANCE
Protein • Foods from animal sources • Dried beans and peas, nuts • Grain products	• Builds and repairs cells • Regulates body processes by providing components for enzymes, hormones, fluid balance, nerve transmission	10–35% • Choose lean sources such as dried beans, fish, poultry, lean cuts of meat, soy, and low-fat dairy products most of the time. • Egg yolks are rich in many nutrients but also high in cholesterol; limit to 5 per week.
Fats All fats are mixtures of saturated and unsaturated (polyunsaturated and mono-unsaturated) types. Polyunsaturated and especially monounsaturated types are considered more desirable because they promote cardiovascular health.	• Supplies essential fatty acids needed for various body processes and to build cell membranes, particularly of the brain and nervous system • Transports certain vitamins	20–35% • Experts disagree about the ideal amount of total fat in the diet. Some say more is fine if it is heart-healthy fat; others recommend limiting total fat. Virtually all experts agree that saturated fat, trans fats, and cholesterol, all of which can raise "bad" (LDL) cholesterol, should be limited.
PRIMARILY SATURATED • Foods from animal sources (meat fat, butter, cheese, cream) • Coconut, palm, palm kernel oils	• Raises blood levels of "bad" (LDL) cholesterol	• Limit saturated fat.
PRIMARILY POLYUNSATURATED (PUFA) • Omega-3 fatty acids: herring, salmon, mackerel, lake trout, sardines, sword fish, nuts, flaxseed, canola oil, soy bean oil, tofu • Omega-6: vegetable oils such as corn, soybean, and safflower (abundant in the American diet)	• Reduces inflammation; influences blood clotting and blood vessel activity to improve blood flow	• Eat fish at least twice a week. • Substitute PUFA for saturated fat or trans fat when possible.
PRIMARILY MONOUNSATURATED (MUFA) Olive oil, canola oil, sesame oil, avocados, almonds, chicken fat	• Raises blood levels of "good" (HDL) cholesterol	• Substitute MUFA for saturated fat or trans fat when possible.
DIETARY CHOLESTEROL Foods from animal sources (egg yolks, organ meats, cheese, fish roe, meat)	• A structural component of cell membranes and some hormones	• The body makes cholesterol, and some foods contain dietary cholesterol. U.S. food labels list cholesterol values.
Trans fat Processed foods, purchased baked goods, margarine and shortening	• Raises blood levels of "bad" (LDL) cholesterol	• U.S. food labels list trans fats.

FAT-SOLUBLE VITAMINS AND FOOD SOURCES	FUNCTIONS	DAILY RECOMMENDED INTAKES FOR ADULTS*
Vitamin A Dairy products, deep yellow-orange fruits and vegetables, dark green leafy vegetables, liver, fish, fortified milk, cheese, butter	• Promotes growth and healthy skin and hair • Helps build strong bones and teeth • Works as an antioxidant that may reduce the risk of some cancers and other diseases • Helps night vision • Increases immunity	700 mcg for women 900 mcg for men
Vitamin D Fortified milk, salmon, sardines, herring, butter, liver, fortified cereals, fortified margarine	• Builds bones and teeth • Enhances calcium and phosphorus absorption and regulates blood levels of these nutrients	5–10 mcg
Vitamin E Nuts and seeds, vegetable and seed oils (corn, soy, sunflower), whole-grain breads and cereals, dark green leafy vegetables, dried beans and peas	• Helps form red blood cells • Improves immunity • Prevents oxidation of LDL cholesterol • Works as an antioxidant that may reduce the risk of some cancers	15 mg
Vitamin K Dark green leafy vegetables, liver, carrots, asparagus, cauliflower, cabbage, wheat bran, wheat germ, eggs	• Needed for normal blood clotting • Promotes protein synthesis for bone, plasma, and organs	90 mcg for women 120 mcg for men

WATER-SOLUBLE VITAMINS

	FUNCTIONS	DAILY RECOMMENDED INTAKES FOR ADULTS*
B vitamins Grain products, dried beans and peas, dark green leafy vegetables, dairy products, meat, poultry, fish, eggs, organ meats, milk, brewer's yeast, wheat germ, seeds	• Help the body use carbohydrates (biotin, B_{12}, niacin, pantothenic acid) • Regulate metabolism of cells and energy production (niacin, pantothenic acid) • Keep the nerves and muscles healthy (thiamin) • Protect against spinal birth defects (folate) • Protect against heart disease (B_6, folate)	• B_6: 1.3–1.5 mg • B_{12}: 2.4 mcg (B_{12} is found only in animal-based food sources; vegetarians need supplements.) • Biotin: 30 mcg • Niacin: 14 mg niacin equivalents for women; 16 mg for men • Pantothenic acid: 5 mg • Riboflavin: 1.1 mg for women; 1.3 mg for men • Thiamin: 1.1 mg for women; 1.2 mg for men
Vitamin C Many fruits and vegetables, especially citrus fruits, broccoli, tomatoes, green bell peppers (capsicums), melons, strawberries, potatoes, papayas	• Helps build body tissues • Fights infection and helps heal wounds • Helps body absorb iron and folate • Helps keep gums healthy • Works as an antioxidant	75 mg for women 90 mg for men

Sources: Institute of Medicine reports, 1999–2001

*mcg=micrograms; mg=milligrams

MINERALS** AND FOOD SOURCES	FUNCTIONS	DAILY RECOMMENDED INTAKES FOR ADULTS*
Calcium Dairy products (especially hard cheese, yogurt, and milk), fortified juices, sardines and canned fish eaten with bones, shellfish, tofu (if processed with calcium), dark green leafy vegetables	• Helps build bones and teeth and keep them strong • Helps heart, muscles, and nerves work properly	1,000–1,200 mg
Iron Meat, fish, shellfish, egg yolks, dark green leafy vegetables, dried beans and peas, grain products, dried fruits	• Helps red blood cells carry oxygen • Component of enzymes • Strengthens immune system	18 mg for women 8 mg for men
Magnesium Nuts and seeds, whole-grain products, dark green leafy vegetables, dried beans and peas	• Helps build bones and teeth • Helps nerves and muscles work properly • Necessary for DNA and RNA • Necessary for carbohydrate metabolism	310–320 mg for women 400–420 mg for men
Phosphorus Seeds and nuts, meat, poultry, fish, dried beans and peas, dairy products, whole-grain products, eggs, brewer's yeast	• Helps build strong bones and teeth • Has many metabolic functions • Helps body get energy from food	700 mg
Potassium Fruit, vegetables, dried beans and peas, meat, poultry, fish, dairy products, whole grains	• Helps body maintain water and mineral balance • Regulates heartbeat and blood pressure	2,000 mg suggested; no official recommended intake
Selenium Seafood, chicken, organ meats, brown rice, whole-wheat (wholemeal) bread, peanuts, onions	Works as an antioxidant with vitamin E to protect cells from damage • Boosts immune function	55 mg
Zinc Oysters, meat, poultry, fish, soybeans, nuts, whole grains, wheat germ	• Helps body metabolize proteins, carbohydrates, and alcohol • Helps wounds heal • Needed for growth, immune response, and reproduction	8 mg for women 11 mg for men

** The following minerals are generally sufficient in the diet when the minerals listed above are present: chloride, chromium, copper, fluoride, iodine, manganese, molybdenum, sodium, and sulfur. For information on functions and food sources, consult a nutrition book.

Nutritional values

The recipes in this book have been analyzed for significant nutrients to help you evaluate your diet and balance your meals throughout the day. Using these calculations, along with the other information in this book, you can create meals that have the optimum balance of nutrients. Having the following nutritional values at your fingertips will help you plan healthful meals.

Keep in mind that the calculations reflect nutrients per serving unless otherwise noted. Not included in the calculations are ingredients that are optional or added to taste, or those that are suggested as an alternative or substitution in the recipe, recipe note, or variation. For recipes that yield a range of servings, the calculations are for the middle of that range. Many recipes call for a specific amount of salt and also suggest seasoning food to taste; however, if you are on a low-sodium diet, it is prudent to omit salt. If you have particular concerns about any nutrient needs, consult your doctor.

The numbers for all nutritional values have been rounded using the guidelines required for reporting nutrient levels in the "Nutrition Facts" panel on U.S. food labels.

The best way to acquire the nutrients your body needs is through food. However, a balanced multivitamin-mineral supplement or a fortified cereal that does not exceed 100 percent of the daily need for any nutrient is a safe addition to your diet.

WHAT COUNTS AS A SERVING?	HOW MANY SERVINGS DO YOU NEED EACH DAY?		
	For a 1,600-calorie-per-day diet (children 2–6, sedentary women, some older adults)	For a 2,200-calorie-per-day diet (children over 6, teen girls, active women, sedentary men)	For a 2,800-calorie-per-day diet (teen boys, active men)
Fruit Group 1 medium whole fruit such as apple, orange, banana, or pear ½ cup (2–3 oz/60–90 g) chopped, cooked, or canned fruit ¼ cup (3 oz/90 g) dried fruit ¾ cup (6 fl oz/180 ml) fruit juice	2	3	4
Vegetable Group 1 cup (1 oz/30 g) raw, leafy vegetables ½ cup (2–3 oz/60–90 g) other vegetables, cooked or raw ¾ cup (6 fl oz/180 ml) vegetable juice	3	4	5
Bread, Cereal, Rice, and Pasta Group 1 slice of bread 1 cup (6 oz/180 g) ready-to-eat cereal ½ cup (2.5 oz/80 g) cooked cereal, rice, pasta	6	9	11

Adapted from USDA Dietary Guidelines (2005).

Purple & blue		CALORIES	PROTEIN/ GM	CARBS/ GM	TOT. FAT/ GM	SAT. FAT/ GM	CHOL/ MG	FIBER/ GM	SODIUM/ MG
p. 23	Blackberry crumble	517	7	79	22	11	34	8	30
p. 23	Raisin & cashew truffles (1 truffle)	70	1	8	4	2	0	1	10
p. 24	Lavender flans	183	8	25	6	3	142	0	94
p. 27	Blueberry coffee cake with crunchy walnut topping	370	5	47	19	9	61	2	185
p. 30	Blackberry granita & cream parfait	257	1	50	7	4	24	1	17
p. 30	Sautéed plums with amaretto	197	2	39	3	2	8	2	25
p. 33	Prune compote with greek-style yogurt	384	4	86	1	1	5	3	47
p. 34	Purple grape tart	252	5	40	8	5	114	1	52

Green		CALORIES	PROTEIN/ GM	CARBS/ GM	TOT. FAT/ GM	SAT. FAT/ GM	CHOL/ MG	FIBER/ GM	SODIUM/ MG
p. 41	Spiced apple cake	310	3	52	11	7	50	2	282
p. 41	Green tea punch	94	1	24	0	0	0	1	4
p. 42	Kiwifruit sorbet	120	1	30	0	0	0	2	10
p. 42	Silky lime mousse	198	6	17	13	7	144	0	70
p. 45	Baked apples with caramel sauce	373	1	82	7	3	10	4	35
p. 45	Stuffed green pears	340	5	69	8	1	0	8	24
p. 48	Kiwifruit tart with lime curd filling	490	6	55	29	17	191	2	66
p. 51	Minted green tea jellies with kiwifruit	81	2	19	0	0	0	1	7

White & tan		CALORIES	PROTEIN/ GM	CARBS/GM	TOT. FAT/ GM	SAT. FAT/ GM	CHOL/MG	FIBER/GM	SODIUM/ MG
p. 57	Ginger angel food cakes	230	4	54	0	0	0	0	114
p. 58	Caramelized bananas	250	2	44	9	6	23	2	14
p. 58	Sauternes-poached pears	413	1	66	0	0	0	5	15
p. 61	Crystallized-ginger gingerbread	223	3	41	5	3	50	1	148
p. 61	White nectarines with lychees and grapes	142	1	36	0	0	0	2	3
p. 64	Fresh dates with pistachio-mascarpone filling	367	6	54	17	8	36	6	27
p. 64	Brandied baked figs	195	1	37	0	0	0	4	2
p. 67	White peach crostatas	313	5	47	12	7	31	2	28
p. 67	Sweet corn bread	498	9	75	18	2	62	4	519
p. 68	Streusel banana muffins	273	4	47	9	5	19	3	263

Yellow & orange		CALORIES	PROTEIN/ GM	CARBS/GM	TOT. FAT/ GM	SAT. FAT/ GM	CHOL/MG	FIBER/GM	SODIUM/ MG
p. 75	Meyer lemon meringue ice cream	284	3	43	13	8	47	0	45
p. 75	Orange & sabayon gratin	265	3	42	5	3	113	4	11
p. 76	Papaya & mango tapioca	193	1	42	3	3	0	2	13
p. 76	Honey-glazed pineapple	143	1	38	0	0	0	2	2
p. 79	Roasted apricot & vanilla tart	258	4	40	9	6	23	2	28
p. 82	Carrot cupcakes with mascarpone icing	373	4	48	19	11	91	1	236
p. 85	Golden kiwifruit pavlovas	350	4	58	13	8	47	2	75
p. 86	Lemon soufflés	112	1	28	0	0	0	0	19
p. 86	Sweet potato pie	310	5	39	16	9	106	2	180
p. 89	Golden fruit bowl with allspice syrup	90	1	23	0	0	0	2	6
p. 89	Golden cherry clafoutis	207	6	35	4	2	111	2	77

Red		CALORIES	PROTEIN/ GM	CARBS/GM	TOT. FAT/ GM	SAT. FAT/ GM	CHOL/MG	FIBER/GM	SODIUM/ MG
p. 95	Berry & ricotta trifles	522	12	88	14	7	140	3	182
p. 96	Plum cake	431	4	50	24	15	113	2	143
p. 96	Raspberry jellies	97	1	23	0	0	0	3	5
p. 99	Cherries flambéed in rum	298	2	51	6	4	13	2	10
p. 99	Rhubarb fool	319	2	31	22	14	82	1	25
p. 102	Brandied berry crepes	182	4	27	5	3	62	3	96
p. 105	Pear & frangipane galettes	584	9	57	37	17	137	6	54
p. 105	Raspberries in red wine syrup	283	1	54	1	0	0	6	7
p. 106	Ruby grapefruit sorbet	156	2	38	0	0	0	0	17
p. 106	Red currant filo tarts	198	2	29	9	5	20	2	93

Brown		CALORIES	PROTEIN/ GM	CARBS/GM	TOT. FAT/ GM	SAT. FAT/ GM	CHOL/MG	FIBER/GM	SODIUM/ MG
p. 113	Prune panforte	210	4	31	9	1	0	3	3
p. 113	Brazil nut & almond torte	248	6	33	12	3	0	3	110
p. 114	Almond cake with kirsch syrup	220	6	33	7	1	115	1	75
p. 117	Hazelnut macaroons (1 macaroon)	41	1	7	1	0	0	0	14
p. 117	Real hot chocolate	335	11	39	20	11	20	3	100
p. 120	Chocolate-pumpkin cake	357	5	55	14	9	51	2	246
p. 120	Pistachio rice pudding	394	13	61	11	5	25	3	116
p. 123	Oatmeal pear crisp	394	5	65	15	9	36	7	88
p. 123	Bread puddings	247	8	30	11	5	122	2	147
p. 124	Walnut & date tart	288	5	42	13	4	66	2	56
p. 124	Polenta cake	313	4	28	20	5	40	2	78

Glossary

almonds: Like most nuts, almonds contain folate, riboflavin, and magnesium; they are also high in omega-3 fatty acids and vitamin E, an antioxidant that protects brain cells, promotes heart health, and lowers LDL (bad) cholesterol.

antioxidant: A substance that intercepts free radicals. Free radicals are unstable oxygen molecules created as our bodies process oxygen. Free radicals injure our other cells and promote damage and diseases ranging from cataracts and wrinkles to cancer and heart disease.

apples: The major portion of the apple's nutrition is in its skin, which contains the flavonoid quercetin, an antioxidant that fights viruses and allergies and is thought to be an anticarcinogenic. Apple flesh is an important source of pectin, a fiber that lowers cholesterol.

apricots: The apricot's color is due to the pigments beta-carotene and lycopene, which promote eye health and heart health, lower the risk of some cancers, and strengthen the immune system. Apricots are also high in vitamin C, potassium, and fiber.

avocados: Technically a fruit, the avocado is high in fat, but most of it is monounsaturated, which helps to lower cholesterol. It also contains beta-sitosterol, a plant cholesterol that lowers cholesterol as well, and may prevent the growth of cancer cells. Avocados are high in vitamins and minerals, especially vitamin A, C, folate, B$_6$, and potassium.

bananas: Bananas are high in potassium, which helps to regulate blood pressure, and may reduce arterial plaque formation and prevent strokes by lowering platelet activity and reducing blood clots. Bananas are also high in vitamins C and B$_6$ and contain a kind of fiber that may protect against colon cancer.

blackberries: Their dark purple color is caused by anthocyanins, which help to lower the risk of some cancers and promote urinary tract health. Second only to blueberries in antioxidant content, they are also high in vitamin C, potassium, folate, and fiber. Varieties include marionberries, loganberries, boysenberries, and olallieberries.

blueberries: These native North American berries are so high in antioxidant and anti-inflammatory compounds that they are considered "brain food": they contain a range of anthocyanins, which are thought to help fight the damaging effects of aging on the brain. Blueberries are available fresh, dried, and frozen.

Brazil nuts: Like all nuts, Brazil nuts are high in protein, fiber, minerals, and vitamin E, but their real claim to fame is their high proportion of selenium, a cancer-fighting antioxidant.

butter: An essential dairy product, butter is made by churning or agitating cream until the fats separate from the liquids and develop a semisolid form. Butter is sold in two basic styles. More familiar is salted butter; for cooking and baking, however, most recipes call for unsalted butter. Unsalted butter lacks the additional salt that can interfere with the taste of the final recipe, and it is also likely to be fresher since salt often acts as a preservative, prolonging butter's shelf life. For the best quality, seek out European-style butter, which contains less moisture and more flavorful butterfat. If you cannot find unsalted butter, salted butter will work in most recipes; just taste and adjust the salt in the recipe as needed. To store unsalted butter that won't be used within a week or so, wrap it in freezer-weight plastic and freeze.

carrots: One carrot provides a whopping 330 percent of the Daily Value of vitamin A, which is the source of its fame as a protector of vision. Carrots are also high in fiber and in bioflavonoids and carotenoids that lower the risk of some cancers, protect the heart, and boost immunity. Maroon and purple carrots contain antioxidants that promote healthy aging.

cashews: Although they are higher in fat than many other nuts, cashews also contain magnesium and copper along with the other usual beneficial compounds of nuts, such as protein and vitamin E.

cherries: Tart red and sweet, dark red cherries derive their color from anthocyanin pigments and other antioxidants, which help to protect the heart and brain, lower the risk of some cancers, and are powerful anti-inflammatories. Both sweet and tart cherries also contain a terpenoid that prevents the growth of tumors.

chestnuts: Although far lower in fat than other nuts (8 percent calories from fat, as opposed to the more than 75 percent of most nuts), chestnuts are, like other nuts, high in protein, minerals, and cancer-fighting antioxidants in the form of flavonoids.

chocolate: Because it is a plant food, chocolate also contains phytochemicals, in the form of a group of antioxidants called catechins, also found in red wine. Dark chocolate is higher in these flavonoids (and lower in fat and sugar) than milk chocolate.

coffee: Like all plant foods, coffee contains beneficial phytochemicals. It is also high in the stimulant caffeine, which some people are sensitive to but which is being studied for its effects countering Parkinson's disease and diabetes.

corn: Corn is rich in vitamins, minerals, protein, and fiber. Yellow corn is given its color by carotenoids that not only fight heart disease and cancer, but also protect against a type of damage to the eye called macular degeneration.

cranberries: High in both fiber and vitamin C, cranberries are excellent for preventing urinary tract infections due to their polyphenols. The anthocyanins that make cranberries red have antioxidant properties that protect the heart and may guard against cancer. Fresh, frozen, and dried cranberries, as well as cranberry juice, are all equally beneficial to health.

cream, whipping (double): When whipping cream, begin by chilling your equipment, including a metal bowl and the beaters, and use well-chilled heavy (double) cream to yield the best results. Using an electric mixer on medium-high speed, beat cream until thick before adding sweetener, such as powdered (icing) sugar, if using. "Soft peaks" means the cream forms peaks that gently slump to one side when the beaters are turned upright. Cream should not be whipped past the soft peak stage, or it will turn into butter. Use the cream immediately after whipping.

currants: Fresh currants are small red or black berrylike fruits grown and used widely in Europe, while dried currants are actually Zante grapes, tiny raisins with a distinctively tart-sweet flavor. If they are unavailable, substitute raisins. Both currants and red grapes contain phenolic compounds, which may reduce the risk of heart disease and certain types of cancer.

dates: Occasionally available fresh in late summer and early fall, dates are more commonly found dried, when their high sugar content increases greatly. They provide iron and protein.

figs: Whether eaten fresh (available in summer and early fall) or dried, figs provide phosphorus, calcium, and iron. They also deliver different phytochemicals according to the color of their skin—purple, tan, or green.

flambéing: Pouring liquor over a dish and igniting it is an essential step in many French dishes. To flambé safely, pour the liquor into a pan safely away from the heat. Briefly place the pan on the heat to warm the liquor, then remove it from the heat once more. Make sure flammable objects are moved away, and use a long kitchen match to flambé. Once the match is lit, hold it just above the liquor to ignite the flames (you are lighting the fumes rising from the heated liquor). The flame should burn out in 30 seconds. Keep a pot lid nearby to smother the flames if they don't subside within a minute.

flour, all-purpose (plain): All-purpose flour is the popular general-use flour that is good for a wide range of desserts. It is made from a mixture of refined soft and hard wheats.

flour, cake (soft-wheat): Low in protein and high in starch, cake flour is milled from soft wheat and contains cornstarch (cornflour). It is fine-textured and has also undergone a bleaching process that increases its ability to hold water and sugar. Cakes made with cake flour have a particularly tender crumb.

ginger: Long prized in Chinese cuisine for its culinary and medicinal uses, ginger aids digestion, reduces nausea, and lowers cholesterol. It contains both antioxidant and antimicrobial compounds.

gooseberries: Available only briefly during the summer months in the United States, gooseberries are more popular in northern Europe. They are high in both vitamin C and fiber.

grapefruit: Half a grapefruit provides 70 percent of the Daily Value of vitamin C. Pink or red grapefruit is high in vitamin A as well. All colors contain flavonoids that help to guard against cancer, while the red type also offers lycopene, another cancer-fighting antioxidant.

grapes: The dark purple Concord grape, which is usually made into grape juice, is extremely high in antioxidants, making grape juice an

important heart-healthy food. Red table grapes also promote heart health and immunity, and green grapes can help lower cancer risk and promote eye health.

green (spring) onions: Like all onions, green onions contain organosulfur compounds, which are thought to protect the heart and improve the ratio of good to bad cholesterol.

guavas: Guava is a rich source of vitamin C. It contains 3 to 6 times more vitamin C than oranges, 10 to 30 times more than bananas, and about 10 times more than papaya. Guavas are also a useful source of calcium, nicotinic acid, phosphorous, and soluble fiber. They are very good for the immune system and are beneficial in reducing cholesterol and protecting the heart.

hazelnuts (filberts): These flavorful nuts are especially high in vitamin E and contain a wide range of imporant minerals as well as dietary fiber.

herbs, green: Not only are fresh herbs rich in the phytochemicals that give them their color and taste, they are important flavor enhancers for all vegetables and some fruits as well.

honey: Available in a range of flavors, from mild clover to intense chestnut, depending on the source of the pollen used by the bees to make this sweetener. The color of a specific honey, from pale to dark, is a clue to the strength of its flavor. Raw, unfiltered honey contains minerals and also retains some pollen, but some individuals may have sensitivities to it in this form.

kiwifruits: Extremely high in vitamin C (two kiwifruits contain 240 percent of Daily Value, almost twice as much as an orange), these fruits are also high in folate and potassium.

kumquats: These tiny oval orange citrus fruits are like backward oranges: their peel is sweet and their flesh is sour. Often candied or used sliced as an accent or whole or sliced as garnish, they are high in vitamin A, vitamin C, and potassium.

lavender: Long used as a calmative, lavender is also a traditional Provençal culinary herb. It contains numerous phytochemicals, including perillyl alcohol, which apparently slows the growth of tumors and destroys cancer cells.

lemons: High in vitamin C, lemons are a flavor enhancer; add lemon juice to raw and cooked fruits and use it to replace salt at the table for vegetables and fish.

lime leaves, Kaffir: These aromatic leaves are used widely in Indian and Southeast Asian cooking. Look for them in specialty food shops and Asian markets. They are harder to find fresh than freeze-dried.

limes: High in vitamin C, like all citrus fruits, lime juice also contains lutein, which benefits eye health. The Persian lime is widely available, while the yellowish green Key lime is usually found fresh only in Florida and some specialty produce markets.

lychees: This fruit of Chinese origin is walnut-sized, with a bumpy red shell encasing white translucent pulp similar in texture to a grape. Lychees are very juicy, with a sweet flavor. Fresh lychees are available from May to July, and canned lychees are available year-round in Asian markets.

macadamia nuts: Macadamias are similar to other nuts in their fiber and beneficial omega-3 fatty acid content, and also contain phytosterols, which reduce LDL (bad) cholesterol and so promote heart health.

mangoes: This colorful orange tropical fruit is extremely high in vitamin A (160 percent of Daily Value) and vitamin C (95 percent of Daily Value). Mangoes also contain beta-carotene as well as quercetin, both of which are thought to fight cancer.

maple syrup: The New England colonists learned from local tribes of Native Americans how to tap maple trees for their sap and boil it down to make a sweetener. Grade A syrup, sometimes called Grade AA, is clear gold and has a mild, delicate flavor that complements waffles and pancakes. Grade B syrup is darker and has a richer, caramel-like flavor. Its stronger taste makes it more suitable for cooking.

melons: Higher in healthful nutrients than any other melon, the cantaloupe is also rich in vitamins A and C and potassium. It is heart-healthy and helps to lower the risk of cancer, thanks to its beta-carotene content. A wide variety of other orange-fleshed melons are also available. Green-fleshed honeydew melons and Persian melons contain cancer-fighting phytochemicals as well.

molasses: The dark residue of the sugar-making process, molasses comes in three forms: light, dark, and blackstrap. Although blackstrap molasses has been touted as highly nutritious, it is little more so than dark molasses, which is more palatable and similarly contains iron, calcium, and phosphorus.

nectarines: Not a hybrid but a relative of the peach, the nectarine has the advantage of an edible skin that contains many of its phytochemicals. Yellow nectarines contain beta-carotene, while the pink-skinned, white-fleshed variety has its own group of beneficial compounds.

oats: Oat groats are whole grains that may be cut into pieces to make Scotch, steel-cut, or Irish oats, or steamed and rolled into old-fashioned, or rolled, oats. When the groats are cut into pieces and rolled thinner, they become quick-cooking oats. All of these forms retain their selenium and cholesterol-fighting nutrients, unlike instant oats. They are also high in vitamins B_1, B_6, and E.

oil, canola: This bland-flavored oil is pressed from rapeseed, a relative of the mustard plant.

High in monounsaturated fat and neutral in flavor, it is a good choice for general cooking and baking.

oranges: Famed for their vitamin C content, oranges are also high in folate and potassium, as well as providing limonoids and flavonoids, both disease-fighting antioxidants.

papayas: With flesh ranging from yellow to orange to red, depending on their type, papayas are high in antioxidant carotenoids, which guard against certain cancers.

passion fruit: Named by a missionary for the Passion of Christ rather than for any earthly romantic feelings, this aromatic fruit has a tart, tropical flavor. Passion fruits are ripe when their inedible skins are wrinkled. Choose one that feels heavy for its size. The pulp and seeds are the parts you eat.

peaches: While its fuzzy skin is usually not eaten, the yellow or white flesh of the peach contains the vitamins A and C and is available fresh, dried, frozen, and canned.

peanuts: Although they are not truly nuts, but legumes, peanuts are high in fat. They are a good source of protein, though they should be eaten in small amounts. Like most nuts, the fat they contain is largely monounsaturated.

pears: The beneficial pigments of pears are concentrated in their skin; as the skin is quite thin (except in the tan-skinned varieties), they can be eaten unpeeled, whether raw or cooked. The flesh contains vitamin A, as well as some phosphorus.

pecans: These nuts are rich in vitamin A and E, as well as heart-healthy sterols.

persimmons: Both the small, squat Fuyu, which is eaten when hard and crisp, and the larger, slightly pointed Hachiya, which is eaten fully ripe, are rich in beta-carotene and vitamin C.

phytochemicals: These natural compounds found in plants impart colors, flavors, and scents to the plant to attract insects and animals that help the plant reproduce or ward off predators. Some phytochemicals help protect the plant against environmental dangers such as radiation from the sun or viruses and other diseases. When these compounds are ingested by humans or animals, they continue to carry out these same functions, preventing damage to cells and diseases and boosting the immune system.

pineapples: The pineapple's sweet, juicy flesh provides manganese, vitamins A and C, and bromelain, an anti-inflammatory enzyme that also acts as a digestive aid.

pine nuts: Delicate, buttery pine nuts contain both iron and thiamin. Used in both Mexican and Italian cooking, they can also be a flavorful garnish for salads and cooked foods.

pistachios: The sweet, pale green flesh of this nut contains potassium and vitamin B6. Look for unsalted shelled pistachios in bulk in natural foods stores. Their papery skins can be removed after toasting by rubbing them in a towel, as with hazelnuts.

plums: The edible skin of the plum, which comes in a variety of colors, contains most of its phytochemicals, though the yellow, purple, or red flesh also has beneficial compounds. A good source of vitamin C, plums are one of the most healthful fruits.

poaching: Cooking in liquid at a temperature just below the boiling point, poaching is a gentle method that works well for delicate foods like fruit. The poaching liquid is sometimes reduced to make a sauce. Heating fruit along with the poaching liquid, rather than adding it to an already-simmering mixture, causes the flavor of the fruit to infuse the syrupy liquid. Once the liquid comes to a boil, reduce the heat as needed to maintain a gentle simmer, with slow bubbles breaking the surface.

polenta: Although polenta is sometimes made from other dried grains or white corn, usually it is coarsely or finely ground yellow cornmeal. Stone-ground cornmeal is higher in quality but also perishable; store it in an airtight container in the refrigerator.

pomegranates: The fleshy seeds of this fruit are high in vitamin C, potassium, and heart-healthy anthocyanins. The fruit is in season during the fall months, while pomegranate juice is available year-round in natural foods stores and some other markets.

prunes: These dried prune plums, now also called dried plums, are rich in vitamin A, potassium, and fiber. They are higher in antioxidants than any other fruit or vegetable, making them the top anti-aging food.

pumpkins: The flesh of the pumpkin is nutrient rich with vitamin A and carotenoids, specifically the cancer-fighters alpha- and beta-carotene and lutein. Choose pumpkins that are unblemished and heavy for their size.

pumpkin seeds: High in fiber, protein, and various minerals, pumpkin seeds also contain beta-sitosterol, which lowers cholesterol and slows the growth of abnormal cells. Clean and toast your own, or buy them in natural foods stores or Latino markets, where they are known as *pepitas*.

quinces: Although it bears a resemblance to an apple or pear, the quince is not a fruit that can be eaten out of hand. Its uncooked flesh is dry in texture and astringent in taste. However, when slowly cooked, a quince will develop an aromatic scent and delightfully mellow flavor. Raw quince may be pale green like a Granny Smith apple or yellow like a Golden Delicious, but takes on a pink to ruby hue as it cooks and red phytochemicals develop in its flesh.

raisins: Antioxidant rich, raisins are also high in vitamins, minerals, and fiber. Both dark and golden raisins (sultanas) start as green grapes, but golden raisins are treated with sulfur dioxide to prevent oxidation.

raspberries: Red raspberries have more fiber than most other fruits; they are also high in vitamin C and folate, and extremely high in cancer-fighting antioxidants. Golden raspberries are less common, but they contain heart- and eye-health bioflavonoids. Although fresh raspberries are fragile, frozen unsweetened raspberries retain their flavor and are available year-round.

rhubarb: These tart red stalks are one of the first signs of spring when they appear in the market. High in vitamin A and beneficial phytochemicals, rhubarb helps to protect the heart, boost immunity, and lower the risk of some cancers.

sesame seeds: Flat and minute, sesame seeds come in several colors, but are most commonly a light ivory. They are rich in minerals such as manganese, copper, and calcium and also contain cholesterol-lowering lignans. Because they have a high oil content, they should be kept refrigerated. Toasting brings out their nutty flavor.

strawberries: Rich in antioxidant content, partly due to their anthocyanin pigments, strawberries are also extremely high in vitamin C. Because of these compounds, as well as their phenolic acids, these berries are thought to be important cancer fighters.

sugar: The most common sugar is granulated white sugar, which has been extracted from sugarcane or beets and refined by boiling, centrifuging, chemical treatment, and straining. For baking recipes, buy only sugar that is labeled cane sugar; beet sugar may have an unpredictable effect. Most sugars marketed as "raw" are actually partially refined. Turbinado, a common raw sugar, has light brown, coarse crystals. Demerara and Barbados are also varieties of raw sugar.

sugar, brown: Rich in flavor, brown sugar is granulated sugar colored with molasses. It has a soft, moist texture and comes in mild-flavored light brown and strong-flavored dark brown varieties.

sugar, superfine (caster): When finely ground, granulated sugar becomes superfine sugar, also known as caster or castor sugar. Because it dissolves rapidly, it is preferred for delicate mixtures such as beaten egg whites and cold recipes such as mixed drinks (it is also sold as bar sugar). It is ideal for making candied citrus peel because the sugar will coat the peel evenly. To make your own, process granulated sugar in a food processor until finer granules form.

sunflower seeds: Nutty-flavored sunflower seeds are rich in iron and protein and may be added to breads and other baked goods or used as a nutritious garnish to add texture to many dishes.

sweet potatoes: The most commonly available of these root vegetables are a pale yellow variety and a dark orange one (often erroneously referred to as a yam, which is in fact a completely different vegetable not widely available in the Unied States). Both are high in fiber, vitamins A and C, and a host of other vitamins and minerals, as well as more beta-carotene than any other vegetable.

tea, green: Green tea is made from steamed and dried tea leaves that (unlike the leaves for black tea) have not been fermented. Both kinds of tea are rich in phytochemicals and appear to fight cardiovascular disease, including stroke, and cancers of the gastrointestinal tract and, surprisingly, skin. And green tea's delicate flavor translates to a light, refreshing dessert. Though convenient, tea bags do not make the best tea, as the leaves are not able to circulate. For better flavor, seek out high-quality loose tea or powder sold at tea shops or specialty food stores. Avoid common commercial brands, which are made from blends of inferior bits of leaves.

walnuts: With the same high levels of protein and vitamin E as most other nuts, walnuts are also especially rich in omega-3 oils, as well as ellagic acid, which helps to lower the risk of cancer.

watermelon: Despite its high water content, this melon provides vitamins A and C, along with the anthocyanins that give it its color.

wheat, whole: The bran in whole wheat (wholemeal) contains selenium and other minerals, as well as vitamin E. Whole wheat is also an important source of fiber, which is thought to help lower the risk of strokes and heart disease. As with all whole grains, all forms of whole wheat, from wheat germ to flour, should be kept refrigerated.

wine: The colors of red and rosé wines are due to the skins of the purple grapes used to make the wines; because of the way the skins are used in red wine production, red wine contains more beneficial antioxidants called phenolics than grape juice. These phytochemicals are believed to contribute to heart health. Additionally, moderate consumption of alcohol such as wine has been shown to lower the level of bad cholesterol and increase the level of good cholesterol.

Bibliography

The resources below were used in the creation of this book, and are recommended for further reading on the subject of colorful plant foods:

BOOKS

Gollman, Barbara, and Kim Pierce. *The Phytopia Cookbook*. Dallas, Tex.: Phytopia, Inc., 1998.

Green, Eliza. *Field Guide to Produce*. Philadephia: Quirk Books, 2004.

Heber, David, M.D., Ph.D. *What Color Is Your Diet?* New York: Harper Collins, 2001.

Hess, Mary Abbott, L.H.D., M.S., R.D., F.A.D.A; Dana Jacobi; and Marie Simmons. *Williams-Sonoma Essentials of Healthful Cooking*. Menlo Park, Calif.: Oxmoor House, 2003.

Joseph, James A., Ph.D.; Daniel A. Nadeau, M.D.; and Anne Underwood. *The Color Code*. New York: Hyperion, 2002.

Pivonka, Elizabeth, R.D., Ph.D., and Barbara Berry, M.S., R.D. *5 a Day: The Better Health Cookbook*. New York: Rodale, 2002.

Tantillo, Tony, and Sam Gugino. *Eat Fresh, Stay Healthy*. New York: Macmillan General Reference, 1997.

WEBSITES

Centers for Disease Control:
http://www.cdc.gov

National Cancer Institute:
http://www.nci.nih.gov

Produce for Better Health Foundation:
http://www.5aday.org

United States Department of Agriculture:
http://www.usda.gov

University of California, Berkeley, School of Public Health Wellness Letter:
http://www.wellnessletter.com

Index

FREE PRESS

A Division of Simon & Schuster, Inc.
1230 Avenue of the Americas
New York, NY 10020

WILLIAMS-SONOMA

Founder & Vice-Chairman Chuck Williams

WELDON OWEN INC.

Chief Executive Officer John Owen

President and Chief Operating Officer Terry Newell

Chief Financial Officer Christine E. Munson

Vice President International Sales Stuart Laurence

Creative Director Gaye Allen

Publisher Hannah Rahill

Associate Publisher Sarah Putman Clegg

Editor Emily Miller

Editorial Assistant Juli Vendzules

Photo Director and Senior Designer Marisa Kwek

Production Director Chris Hemesath

Color Manager Teri Bell

Production and Reprint Coordinator Todd Rechner

THE WILLIAMS-SONOMA NEW HEALTHY KITCHEN *DESSERTS*

Conceived and produced by Weldon Owen Inc.
814 Montgomery Street, San Francisco, CA 94133
Telephone: 415 291 0100 Fax: 415 291 8841

In collaboration with Williams-Sonoma, Inc.
3250 Van Ness Avenue, San Francisco, CA 94109

A WELDON OWEN PRODUCTION
Copyright © 2006 by Weldon Owen Inc. and Williams-Sonoma Inc.

For information regarding special discounts for bulk purchases,
please contact Simon & Schuster Special Sales at 1-800-456-6798 or
business@simonandschuster.com

Set in Vectora

Color separations by Mission Productions Limited.
Printed and bound in Hong Kong by Midas Printing.

First printed in 2005.

10 9 8 7 6 5 4 3 2 1

Library of Congress Cataloging-in-Publication data is available.

ISBN-13: 978-0-7432-7860-7
ISBN-10: 0-7432-7860-7

ACKNOWLEDGMENTS

Weldon Owen wishes to thank the following people for their generous support in producing this book:
Copy Editor Carolyn Miller; **Consulting Editor** Judith Dunham; **Proofreaders** Desne Ahlers and Carrie Bradley; **Indexer** Ken DellaPenta;
Karen Brux; Adrienne Aquino; Shadin Saah; Carol Hacker; Jackie Mills; Marianne Mitten; and Richard Yu.

Photographer Dan Goldberg

Photographer's Assistant Julie Caine

Food Stylist Jen Straus

Assistant Food Stylist Max La Rivière-Hedrick

Photographer Ben Dearnley

Food and Prop Stylist Julz Beresford

Assistant Food Stylist Jess Sly

The images on the following pages were created by this photo team:
8–9; 18 *top left*; 21; 22; 25; 26; 28 *bottom*; 29; 31; 36; 39; 40; 43;
46 *top*; 47; 49; 52 *top left, bottom left, bottom right*; 62; 63 *bottom*;
69; 70 *top left*; 73; 77; 80; 81 *top*; 83; 84; 87; 90 *bottom left, bottom
right*; 93; 97; 98; 101 *top*; 104; 107; 108 *top left, bottom right*;
112; 118 *top*; 121.

The images on the following pages were created by this photo team:
18 *top right, bottom left, bottom right*; 28 *top*; 32; 35; 44; 46 *bottom*;
50; 52 *top right*; 55; 56; 59; 60; 63 *top*; 65; 66; 70 *top right, bottom left,
bottom right*; 74; 78; 81 *bottom*; 88; 90 *top left, top right*; 94; 100; 101
bottom; 103; 108 *top right, bottom left*; 111; 115; 116; 118 *bottom*;
119; 122; 125.

A NOTE ON WEIGHTS AND MEASURES

All recipes include customary U.S. and metric measurements. Metric conversions are based on
a standard developed for these books and have been rounded off. Actual weights may vary.